My Mother's Quilts
Designs from the Thirties

BY SARA NEPHEW

Illustration from the Montgomery Ward 1933 catalog used with permission of Montgomery Ward & Co., p. 20.

DEDICATION

This book is dedicated to my mother . . . and to all mothers, grandmothers, daughters, and grand-daughters who were willing to share their family history and family photographs with other quilters.

ACKNOWLEDGMENTS

Special thanks to:
Carolann Palmer, who allowed free access to her pattern collection; to Patty Gray, who lent her pattern collection and fabric swatch book; and to Eldra Pebsworth, who provided a Ward's Catalog.

Diane Coombs, Marsha McCloskey, Cleo Nollette, Judy Pollard, Laura Reinstatler, and Christine Russell, who made quilt tops from thirties' fabric for this book.

Molly Barry, Diane Coombs, Pamela Foster, Mary Fox, Dana Graupmann, Judy Hodson, Rose Herrera, Jocelyn Holm, Grace Koenig, Marsha McCloskey, Sylvia McFadden, Mary Meyer, Nina Nicholl, Marina Perecz, Mar Tobiason, Dolores Wagner, and Margaret Zanon who kindly loaned their quilts to be photographed for this book.

CREDITS

Photography by Carl Murray
Illustration and Graphics by Stephanie Benson
Text and Cover Design by Judy Petry

My Mother's Quilts: Designs from the Thirties ©
© Sara Nephew, 1988

Library of Congress Card Number 87-051212
ISBN: 0-943574-47-1

CONTENTS

PREFACE

Times were tough in the thirties. The Great Depression affected everyone. Many people who lived through those years still save string and use a teabag five times. My mother told me of standing across the street from an ice cream parlor and wanting a cone so bad, but because she was newly married and had little money, the five cents for ice cream was just not in the budget. She remembers a neighbor lady, who worked in a bedding factory under a government-sponsored program. She would work all week folding, sorting, and packing nightclothes, sheets, etc., and then at the end of the week, she could choose a pair of pillowcases or maybe a mattress pad for her wage.

Recently, my mother presented me with a large collection of quilt patterns she had clipped from newspapers in the thirties and pasted into a scrapbook—patterns she one day hoped to use. Most of them remained only newspaper clippings. Mother never made all the quilts she dreamed about. But the patterns she saved inspired me to write this book. And now I'm making quilts, some of the quilts she planned to make. That's why I've called this book *My Mother's Quilts.*

Illustration from the Montgomery Ward 1933 catalog used with permission of Montgomery Ward & Co., p. 1.

INTRODUCTION

The first section of this book contains a short historical background of the 1930s. It is neither exhaustive nor detailed, but enough to give you the flavor of the 1930s. Next, the book reveals where to find thirties' quilts and other items, what to do with your find, and how to clean and/or repair it. A guide for identifying fabric is also included.

Then, because many have inherited thirties' quilt tops from grandmothers or aunts, a brief section gives general instructions for quilting. This section also discusses what to do with those unfinished quilts you may find and includes examples of problem solving.

Color photos in the next section detail characteristics of thirties' quilts. Included are tips on identifying these quilts through fabric, color, and patterns.

To give you a greater feeling of these times and what life was really like in the thirties, I've included personal stories of some thirties' quiltmakers, pictured with quilts they have made. This color section features a gallery of quilts and tops either actually made in the thirties or started then and finished now. Also included are some recent quilts inspired or influenced by thirties' fabrics, patterns, or colors.

The final section of the book contains patterns for you to try. Some of the most popular thirties' patterns (Dresden Plate, Nine-Patch, Double Wedding Ring) are not included, because they are familiar and easily can be found in many books.

One of the hallmarks of the thirties was a willingness to experiment and try new patterns. I hope you will want to try some of the thirties' patterns included here. May you find them fun and inspiring!

Illustration from the Montgomery Ward 1933 catalog used with permission of Montgomery Ward & Co., p. 115

HISTORY

The thirties holds a fascination or carries a nostalgia for many of us. Even though we cannot talk about the thirties as if they stood alone, this decade is bracketed by two major events: the stock market crash in 1929 and the beginning of World War II. But the seeds for these events were sown in earlier years.

being done. Silk patches and thread were still being made into Crazy quilts. Embroidery was an important skill. At the same time, the arts and crafts movement was reacting against Victorian clutter and overdecoration, urging simplicity. Artists and teachers were encouraging a colonial revival. Technological, social, and economic changes were

Turn-of-the-century needle packet

Things were changing fast, even at the turn of the century. Victorianism, reaction to it, and all new trends were mixed into what was just ordinary life for everyone. Business was being cleaned up. Muckrakers and unionists were trying to change the extreme divisions between the rich and the poor. "American conscience was to be the dominant phenomenon in American affairs until about 1915"[1] when the First World War began to take shape. People believed things could be better, and they changed laws governing budgets, labor, working conditions, private ownership and exploitation of land, women's vote, advertising, and consumption of alcohol, food, and drugs. One example was the graduated income tax established in 1913.[2]

At the same time, scientists and inventors were changing the world in other ways. Henry Ford introduced America to the automobile. Electricity and mechanical flight were becoming part of life. Plastic, railroads, trolley buses, and popular radio all became part of the mainstream of technology. Then, the First World War added its push to the direction events were taking. It reinforced technological advance, and also, at a distance, helped contribute to the stock market crash, the depression, and World War II, partly by using up money, men, and resources.[3]

These trends in society were echoed in the home, and quilting reflected the influence of these times. In the early 1900s, some Victorian types of handwork were still

causing a nostalgia for simpler times and an appreciation for simplicity of design. This desire for artistic simplicity and a sentimental remembrance of the past could be combined in a quilt.

Needle packet designs from early 1930s (top) and late 1930s (bottom).

A needle packet from World War II era

After the First World War, patriotism and a pride in all things American added to the reasons for making quilts. By the twenties, widespread interest in quiltmaking already existed. Kits were available, quilt patterns were featured in newspapers, and books and pamphlets on quilting were published. Carlie Sexton, a writer who publicized the colonial revival, published *Early American Quilts* in 1924 and *Old Fashioned Quilts* in 1928. Fabrics, fabric pattern designs, and colors were already moving toward the pastels and the imaginative abundance called "thirties fabrics." Then the failure of the stock market in 1929 added an explosive push to the interest in quilts—poverty. Quilting, which was already beautiful, interesting, and fun, became a way to save money.

In 1931 McKim Studios published Ruby McKim's *One Hundred and One Patchwork Patterns*, a compilation of her newspaper columns and a kind of announcement of quilting fever. Other familiar names appeared in magazines and newspapers in the following years, among them Anne Orr and Rose Kretsinger.

Quilting often has been a consolation to ladies with difficult lives, and the thirties were difficult. These women must have looked forward to the weekly quilt patterns in the newspaper, digging through their feedsack bags of fabric scraps and planning something beautiful, when they found a pattern they especially liked. The enjoyment of quilting continued through the rest of the decade, although not as many new and attractive designs were produced in the latter part of the thirties as in the beginning. Perhaps the quilting fervor would have continued longer if not for the war.

World War II took the majority of the effort and attention of the American people. The ferment of a productive period in quiltmaking was over. But we can still enjoy the thirties' designs in our collections and in the quilts and tops we have inherited.

Sources of Thirties' Quilts

Most likely you have had an opportunity to see quilts from the 1930s—many of them are still around. You can find more quilts from this period than you might expect, considering most thirties' quilts were made for use and were worn out. Some were saved, however, and some were never finished. These unfinished ones may be the most promising of all.

Many people inherit unfinished projects from someone: their mother or grandmother, an aunt or an older lady friend. If you haven't been so lucky as to inherit a project, you still have many opportunities to own a thirties' quilt. Try stopping regularly at antique stores, flea markets, and thrift stores. Some people make their finds at garage sales. A certain amount of persistence can reward you with thirties' tops, quilts, and/or fabric.

Even if you have inherited some quilt tops, etc., you may find it worthwhile to obtain additional bits and pieces of fabric for repairs, setting strips, or binding. Old patterns can help you identify your quilts. Even extra-sharp old needles may prove helpful.

Where is the best place to look? Much will depend on your personality. All the sources have their own advantages and drawbacks. For example, when you go to an antique store, someone else has already found lots of old things from garage sales and estate sales, so you don't have to look through bicycles, washing machines, and plastic toys to search for finds. However, usually you will pay the highest prices here. You might find some quilt squares in a bag and get them for twenty dollars. Don't be afraid to look in nooks and crannies, ask the proprietor if he has any old fabric or needlework, or make a lower offer. There's an old saying: It never hurts to ask.

Thrift shops have the advantage of volume. Every week you may find different items on hangers or in racks or piles. Prices vary from outrageous to a steal. Even here you can ask the manager about the price. That sixty-dollar quilt may have been there long enough to qualify for a 20% markdown. Don't forget to check old books and plastic bags full of notions.

Flea markets have been the source of many good finds. These contain various vendors in individual stalls or booths. A cardinal rule of an open-air flea market is to BE EARLY. I must admit, however, flea markets are not

Illustration from the Montgomery Ward 1933 catalog used with permission of Montgomery Ward & Co., p. 20.

my favorite place to shop. Too many other customers are competing with me, and I always seem to run into the seller who wants antique-store prices for plastic junk.

Many people have purchased beautiful quilts, tops, and squares at auctions. An acquaintance bought a very large, exquisitely embroidered and appliquéd Hmong quilt top for seven dollars at an auction, simply because no one else knew what they were looking at. The problem with auctions is you have to wait until an item comes up for bid. Also, you may have to pay more than your original bid, if someone else has their eye on the same thing.

My choice for treasure hunting is a weekly round of the garage sales. For five years I went over a regular route every Saturday morning. That way I could recognize last week's signs that were not taken down and become familiar with the area, so I didn't waste any time getting lost. The most important rule is to be the first one there, even if you only go to one garage sale. Otherwise you'll be hearing about the ones that got away.

One sale I visited on the second day had a cardboard box on the ground and on it was written "QUILT TOPS — $1.50." I tipped it over and flapped it around, but found nothing. I asked the gentleman in charge, a pleasant fellow in his late fifties, "What quilt tops?" He said, "Yeah, I guess those were underpriced. The first lady at the sale bought them all. There were some my mother made and some my grandmother made." I'm still trying to convince myself they were probably poorly made with ugly colors.

Saving a Thirties' Quilt

So your Aunt Lizzie gave you all her old fabric, quilt tops, quilt squares, and a sewing basket. Or you found blocks and tops at a fantastic garage sale. What do you do with these things? Sometimes it's best to think this question over for a while. It's not going to hurt the fabric if it is in proper storage for a few more years. In the meantime, you may be learning the value of what you have and the best use of it.

Evaluate your treasures carefully. Items from the thirties are not yet represented extensively in museums, but what you have may deserve to be in a museum some day. You may be able to build a unique private collection. If what you have is one of a kind, beautiful enough or valuable enough, it may deserve careful conservation and preservation.

How can you tell? Educate yourself. Read books and look at pictures of quilts. Visit museums. If you see some possibility that what you have is of high quality, show it to a museum expert or even to your own quilt guild to get some information. If there is a possibility of antique value, then do not change the condition of the quilt, even as to cleanliness, without professional advice. Professionals can refer you to special cleaning methods and storage. (Items from the thirties, however, are often still strong and clean if they have been stored away.)

Some thirties' quilts and tops, while they may be striking or outstanding, are not museum pieces. These then are relatively simple to evaluate. Quilt squares and unquilted tops could become decorative items without much effort, or they could be made into complete quilts. Ragged or stained pieces of old quilts are quite common, and if they have no historical interest, could be cut down into throws, pillows, or stuffed animals. Quilt tops may be hung on the wall or used as a special tablecloth or throw. Do not attempt to quilt an old top if the fabric feels brittle, if some tears are in evidence, etc. Check for splits, tears, or holes, and gauge the feel of the fabric (see Cleaning and Repair section).

You may find large quantities of all kinds of fabric, thread, zippers, pincushions, needles, pins, buttons, elas-tic, and all kinds of sewing supplies. Other items such as patterns, needle cases, or fabric sample books may be the beginning of a collection, or they may be used as supplies to help you finish quilts and wall hangings. For example, antique needle cases often have very fine needles, which are superior for handwork, if they are not rusty. After setting aside antique fabrics and notions, either to use or as part of a collection, you may be able to outfit a workroom with found objects.

More unusual items, such as a large collection of old iron-on patterns for embroidery or counted cross-stitch or a scrapbook of quilt patterns from the newspaper, might be the beginning of a collection or could be donated to the library or a quilt guild. Old needlework magazines or outdated fabric swatch books are also of interest to many people.

CLEANING AND REPAIR

First decide if you can use the set of blocks, the top, or quilt as it is without changing it. A quilt in good condition can be put on a bed, or with the addition of a sleeve, on the wall. Wash it only as necessary. Once every year or two is often enough, less often if it does not get dirty or is in bad condition.

But if you must wash your quilt, put the quilt in cool water and a mild soap solution in the bathtub and allow it to soak. Agitate it gently with your hands without lifting it out of the tub or wringing it. Then allow it to drain in the tub. Repeat the washing if necessary. Finally, fill the tub with cool water only, rinse the quilt, and allow it to drain as before. Repeat rinse until the water is clear. Allow the quilt to drain in the tub until it is no longer heavy. Then spread the damp quilt across two clotheslines, across some bushes, or flat on a sheet or blanket to dry, preferably in the shade on a warm day. I even wash my brand new quilts this way.

I have made many mistakes cleaning old quilts and ruined my share. Washing old quilts in the washing machine may not reduce them to shreds the first time, but you may be unpleasantly surprised to begin missing pieces the third or the fifth time. Also, do not soak a blood-stained old quilt in hot water and enzyme solutions if you value the integrity of the unstained portions. If you cannot get expert advice on stain removal, wait until a safe method is pointed out. Occasionally, a dye will cause one particular color to rot out in a quilt, or use or abuse will damage part of a quilt or top. These damaged quilts can become cutter quilts. If it is too damaged to drape over a chair or bed, then the best choice is to cut out the good part of the quilt and use it in some way, preferably where it won't get a lot of wear and thus will last longer. A pillow, a stuffed animal, a framed picture, or a Christmas stocking can all display small bits of handiwork.

One common problem you may encounter is rust spots. Certain solutions can change rust spots from the original strong brown to a pale gray. My experience has shown that these solutions don't really take the spots out and may affect the old fabric. Actually, a few light rust spots do little more than assure you it is an old piece. They don't really detract from its beauty. If there are some large, ugly rust spots, your best choice is to replace the affected fabric. The most annoying rust spots are those caused by someone pinning old quilt blocks together, with the oxidized holes going through the whole set of blocks. At least this may teach us not to leave pins in our work!

If you have a number of inherited quilt tops or thrift shop projects ready to quilt, try to sharpen your quilting skills on the least attractive first, and save the best for last. (This can be very hard to do!) In repairing construction problems, the learning process is the same one forced on many young quilters by their mothers or grandmothers in times past. "If it's not right, take it out and do it over again." A word of caution here: bear in mind that too much reworking can damage both new and old materials. So, careful planning is essential for any repair procedure.

Try to do it once and do it right. Having some extra fabric on hand can be very consoling if it doesn't work.

Identifying Fabric

Whether shopping at antique shops, thrift shops, or garage sales, some knowledge of how to evaluate fabrics can be very helpful. Being able to identify 100% cotton can make it easy and inexpensive to build an exciting fabric collection, while looking for old blocks and tops. Found fabrics are not usually on a bolt, and only occasionally will you find a fabric contents sticker still attached. Three main techniques can help identify fabrics if they lack the contents sticker: burning, crumpling, and careful observation. The most revealing test is to burn a small piece of the material.

Cottons display the following signs:

1. They burn smoothly and evenly.
2. They do not have a bad odor when burning.
3. After burning a small corner and blowing out the flame, you should see a soft ash, usually brown, which can be easily and more or less completely crumbled away.
4. After the ash has been crumbled away, the remaining fabric has a soft edge.

Illustration from the Montgomery Ward 1933 catalog used with permission of Montgomery Ward & Co., p. 116.

Polyesters and blends, on the other hand:

1. Burn enthusiastically, in spurts, and with some smoke.
2. Smell like burning plastic.
3. After blowing out the flame, you may see bumps and bubbles of melted plastic that will not crumble, or
4. If the ash does crumble, blends have a hard edge that shows the presence of plastic in the fabric.

The smell of the fabric can occasionally help you identify wool. (Wool often smells of mothballs.) However, the match test is again the sure thing. Burnt wool smells like singed chickens (or burnt hair, if you prefer), stops burning when the match is removed from the fabric, and has an ash that crumbles away easily, leaving a soft edge. Wool blends show the same characteristics as the cotton blends.

Care must be taken when burning fabrics. Very seldom do I ask for a match at a garage sale. It's better to make a small investment and bring the fabric home, where small swatches can be burned over the sink or wood stove. Do not burn cotton over a pile of other fabrics. Be prepared to blow out the burning area before it becomes larger than a quarter. Do not test fabrics where flammable materials are present.

To evaluate fabrics without burning, check these characteristics:

1. Crumple the fabrics. Blouse-weight cotton will wrinkle and stay wrinkled. Some weaves of cotton, however, will not wrinkle as much, including cotton sateen.
2. Cotton feels soft and smooth. Synthetic fabrics are harder and somewhat sticky to the touch. Buying small pieces and taking them home for match-testing will soon allow you to recognize fabric by its feel.
3. Cotton has a different look in shine and color than blends. (Blends are deeper in color with a shine on each individual thread.)

Mistakes will be made, of course, but reselling fabric scraps is usually a relatively easy matter, if you belong to a sewing or needlework group.

Fabric must also be checked for signs of age. Yellowing is acceptable, possibly even desirable. But brittleness makes fabric unusable. Cotton that tears too easily in all directions or even pulls apart in pieces must be thrown out.

When checking a piece before buying it, your eyes are the best tool; looking will not harm someone else's property. Damage is usually visible somewhere on the quilt, in splits and tatters.

Turn a Top into a Quilt

For those of you lucky enough to inherit or find a thirties' top in good condition, these basic instructions should help you finish your quilt. First, check the quilt top for open seams, unsuitable fabric, or other flaws that can be corrected before quilting. Once this is done, obtain a quilt batt and the backing. If you are lucky, you will have a big piece of thirties' cotton sateen for the back that goes with the colors of the top. Sateen is so easy to needle because it's more loosely woven than percale or even muslin. Other good backings are extra-wide woven 100% cotton fabric, so no seams are needed, or unbleached muslin, with lengths pieced to the proper size. Always be sure that the back is 8-10″ larger than the front in each dimension. The quilt batt should also be larger than the top, as large as the back if possible. To give an authentic appearance to a thirties' quilt, use a cotton batt or low-loft (thin) bonded polyester batt. Prewash the backing. Some cotton batts can be presoaked and dried in the dryer. Prewashing makes quilting easier.

MARKING THE QUILT TOP

Choosing a quilting pattern is a difficult decision for many. One easy choice for a thirties' quilt is a grid, since it was commonly used at that time. Or the quilting can follow some of the lines of the piecing or applique. I like to mark the pattern with a ruler or freehand, using a washout chalk pencil (Dixon). A soft lead pencil, used lightly, is also a traditional marking tool. Quilt templates or improvised guides may be used to mark the pattern. If you mark the quilt top before basting, you can work out the design while looking at the whole top, then you can just relax when quilting.

My particular problem is that I often change my mind about which quilt pattern I want to use, even after I have already done some quilting. So for me, safety consists of waiting until I have it in the hoop and marking one small area at a time. I quilt as close as I can force myself, bearing in mind that quilting is most attractive when there is a lot of it. If you are learning on a practice top and using a thin, bonded polyester batt, the quilting lines can be farther apart. A cotton batt requires quilt lines to be 1″ apart. A part-cotton batt can have 2″ between quilt lines.

BASTING THE QUILT

Spread the quilt back, wrong side up, on a large table or on the floor. I use masking tape to keep the quilt back flat on our short nap carpet. Then spread the quilt batt over this, gently stretching it and smoothing out wrinkles. If the batt is too small, add another piece, using a large ladder stitch. Do not overlap the pieces or pull the thread too tight.

Spread the quilt top right side up on top of the batt. Using a large needle and light-colored basting thread, take large running stitches through all three layers in horizontal and vertical rows, starting with a center row. The closer together these rows are, the easier the quilt will be to handle later. Basting rows should be no farther apart than 8-10″. End with a row of basting stitches all the way around the outside edge of the top.

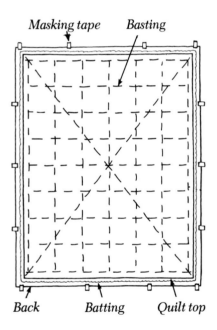

Masking tape   *Basting*

Back   *Batting*   *Quilt top*

QUILTING

Put the basted quilt into a frame or hoop. Then using quilting thread, a thimble, and a quilting needle, take running stitches through all three layers. I use a No. 7 quilting needle because I bend or break needles very easily. Many people use a smaller needle. I stretch the quilt very tightly in hoop or frame and use the thimble to rock the needle back and forth through the three layers of quilt. The middle finger with the thimble pushes the needle, the first finger supports and guides the needle slightly

from the side, and the thumb is out ahead, pushing the fabric down so the needle can come back out. The other hand is underneath, pushing the fabric up so the needle can go in. I average 15-16 stitches to the inch. Some people do beautiful quilting one stitch at a time, putting the needle down through the layers with one hand and back up through the layers with the other hand. And there are other methods too. Whatever method is comfortable for you, practice it and you will improve.

Make a small knot (2 twists of thread), put the needle between the layers 1″ away from where quilting begins, and bring it out on the quilting line. Pull to pop the knot in, take a backstitch, and quilt. When you have a little thread left, take a backstitch, bringing the needle and thread to the top. Wrap the thread twice around the needle, then insert the needle exactly back into the hole it just came out of. Going through just the top layer of fabric, come out an inch away and snip the thread.

BINDING THE QUILT

Cut bias strips of fabric four times the width of finished binding plus 1 1/4″ for the seams and the folds. (1/4″ binding needs a 2 1/4″ strip) Piece strips on the diagonal or perpendicular to a length that is the sum of all sides plus 12″. Press in half lengthwise, wrong sides together. Starting on one side, sew this doubled strip to the front quilt edge, lining up all cut edges.

1. Using 1/4″ seam allowance, sew binding strips to front of quilt, sewing through all layers. Be careful not to stretch binding or quilt edge as you sew. Stitch until you reach the seam line point at corner. Backstitch; cut threads.
2. Turn quilt to prepare for sewing along next edge. Fold binding away from quilt as shown, then fold again to place binding along edge of quilt. (This fold creates an angled pleat at corner.)

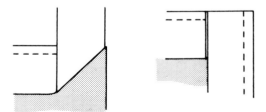

3. Stitch from fold of binding to seam line of adjacent edge. Backstitch; cut threads. Fold binding as in step 2 and continue around edge.
4. Join beginning and ending of binding strip, or han sew one end to overlap other.

5. Turn binding to back side and blindstitch in place. At each corner, fold binding in sequence shown to form a miter on back of quilt.

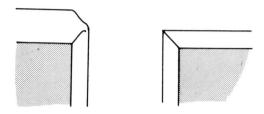

Unfinished Quilts

No matter how pretty quilt squares and antique fabric may be in a pile, there's a continuing urge to make them into a quilt. If it is a family heirloom or one of the many wonderful pieces that belong in a home, not a museum, you will often get the most use and enjoyment out of your finds it they are made into quilts.

However, you may run into problems trying to finish your quilt. Often there's an error or distortion in the blocks, which may be the reason why a particular project was never finished. Sometimes long storage has caused problems that didn't exist originally. Many pieces may need extensive work to be usable. The following pages will address common problems of these old quilts and give some solutions.

DESIGN PROBLEMS

The most obvious kind of problem is often a design problem. It doesn't look good! The quiltmaker might not have sewn the squares together, or may have sewn them together into a top and never quilted it, because she didn't like the way it looked. The overriding design problem in thirties' quilts is too much pattern and too many prints all together. Many thirties' prints are black and white, or a color and white. When you piece these all together, the whole design becomes grayed, oatmealy, and somewhat confusing.

The good qualities of these prints are that they have lots of nostalgic value and are entertaining close up; you can spend lots of time looking at the little individual pattern pieces. If you are dealing with an unfinished project, you can often correct these design problems. The solution is to add something to the design that separates and sets off the highly patterned fabrics. This may be setting strips, plain fabric blocks, or additional pattern blocks in bright or strong solid-color fabric.

DESIGN: SOME EXAMPLES OF PROBLEM SOLVING

ADD CLEAR COLORS

The Nine-Patch quilt shown in color on page 39 was purchased as a top at a garage sale for five dollars. It had two problems. One, it was confused and grayed out from too many patterned fabrics, and secondly, some of the fabrics were extremely gauzy. My inexperience underlined the problems because I washed the quilt top in the washing machine, and many of the fabrics pulled apart at the seams. The design problem and the construction problem were both solved by replacing all of the nine-patch blocks that contained sleazy fabric. Instead, blocks made of bright, strong solid colors from thirties' fabrics were sewed in place. The top was then quilted.

ADD STRONG DESIGN STRUCTURE

Another common design problem results when scraps of solids and prints are used at random in the blocks. Then, when the quiltmaker tries to put the blocks together in a solid set, no clear pattern or design results. To solve this problem, the blocks must be separated with another fabric. Either setting strips or plain blocks would work.

The Blue Baby quilt on page 39 was assembled from scrap squares in two different patterns. Only two additional squares were made with a strong thirties' blue solid and a green and white thirties' print. These two squares and the solid blue border turn this into a very graphic design with fun details in the fabric.

The Fly Foot quilt shown in color on page 45 was made from thirteen blocks. Including twelve plain squares of thirties' green enables the random value changes in the individual blocks to add visual interest to the design, rather than confusion.

ADD AREAS OF DARKER FABRIC

Another extremely common problem with thirties' quilts is the use of too many pastels or too much muslin, resulting in a quilt that looks washed-out while it's still brand-new. Many of these quilts were completely quilted and are part of a collection.

But if one of these too-light unfinished quilts falls into your hands, you may be able to correct the problem. Beautifully colored setting strips between light squares may improve the design. Many embroidered quilts are finished this way, and then the setting becomes the overall design. If working with pieced squares, I think a few squares pieced in stronger colors and mixed with the light quilt blocks would probably be necessary.

The seven Prairie Queen quilt blocks shown below were purchased at a St. Vincent de Paul store for eight dollars. Laying them out together on the floor made it easy to see why the project was never finished. The color in the printed fabrics washes out almost to the point of invisibility because of all the muslin around it. Thirteen more squares were constructed from a stock of thirties' fabrics. Of course, colors were chosen with care to bring out the best in the seven squares already finished. The completed top shown on page 46 fits the text that accompanied the original pattern printed from the thirties: "Pay homage to the 'Prairie Queen,' reigning favorite of patchwork quilters everywhere."

OTHER CREATIVE SOLUTIONS

Many poor design choices caused a project to be abandoned halfway. An example is the Log Chain quilt top shown on this page. This top had shocking pink and

Log Chain quilt top with stripping between the blocks.

Seven Prairie Queen blocks found at St. Vincent de Paul.

gold stripping between the blocks and around the edges. The stripping did not work with the plaids and mellow flour sack fabrics in the blocks. Possibly the person who added the setting strips and border to this quilt was trying to make a few blocks go a long way. Either she was given the blocks or ran out of desire to make more. And she wanted a large quilt. In any case, the color choices for the border are garish with the old flour sack fabrics. I removed the unhappy fabrics and just set the blocks together to complete the design, so that now it looks somewhat like an Irish Chain. The finished top is shown in color on page 43. Often we sacrifice design integrity if we try to make a quilt larger than it really deserves.

One unusual problem was the result of the thirties' desire for new, unusual designs. In a box of fabric scraps was found a bundle of about fifteen unfinished quilt squares. It evidently was a design that was to be partly pieced, and then completed by appliqueing to a background square. It resembled a dandelion with a central stem of dark thirties' green and a fan of leaves on each side in printed fabrics. The quilter had matched the fabrics so that they appeared in the same order on each side

A fabric dandelion with a bright orange circle.

The butterflies are poorly placed on these blocks.

of the stem. On top of the stem was to be attached a very large bright orange circle. Along with the original seamstress, I gave up on the dandelion design. Instead, the leaves were trimmed into a tiny fan and the result became a Fan doll quilt. Placement of the green stem was varied to add interest. (See page 35.) I still have the bright orange disks in my scrap basket of antique fabrics. They'll be just perfect for something.

CONSTRUCTION PROBLEMS

Another reason why a project may have remained unfinished is not as obvious. A few years ago, I traded work on a Crazy quilt for a set of Butterfly blocks. These butterflies had three problems:

1. The quilter had not drawn the design on the background fabric so placement of the parts was often incorrect.
2. The body parts were clumsily cut so they were not consistent in size and shape.
3. Some light thirties' fabrics did not stand out from the muslin background.

To solve these problems, I drew the design on the muslin for uniform placement and added bias strips to clean up the wing shapes and help them stand out. See the results on page 35.

You may unknowingly purchase a construction problem because sometimes it is not as obvious as a design problem. One mistake found often in thirties' quilts is the use of unsuitable material. Because money was tight,

they often used whatever material came to hand. Often weak, thin, or gauzy material was mixed in with good fabrics. If not in the majority, these poor materials should be replaced before the whole piece is quilted. If most of the quilt top is made from insubstantial materials, you can still use it. There is no necessity to use it as a warm bed covering, but it can be hung on the wall.

Of course, inexperienced quiltmakers of the thirties often made the same mistakes inexperienced quiltmakers are liable to make now. You may run into any error — inaccurate piecing, insufficient seams, careless cutting, pooches and puckers, etc. Consider the amount of time repairs will take and balance this against the beauty of appearance or the sentimental value the finished project will have. Perhaps this particular piece should be left in the thrift shop for some other industrious soul to finish.

Some errors can be quilted out and some can't. Only some experience with the amount of time and trouble repairs can take will give you a yardstick to judge by. One true advantage of doing this kind of work is the skills developed by doing repairs. Stitches become smaller and more regular, fabric qualities begin to be recognized, pattern construction is learned. And you learn to make each quilt top as perfectly finished as possible, before quilting, in order to save grief later on.

UTILIZING A FEW BLOCKS

In many of these projects, there were only a few blocks to work with. Often you can draft the pattern and construct more blocks if you have a stock of thirties' material to work with. Sometimes you can use a solid or muslin to fill in the needed spaces. The fabric stores and quilt shops do have some solid colors that match thirties' fabrics. Concord Fabrics has produced "That Green,"

#343-65615, especially to match thirties' green. I have used it with excellent results. Also useful is "Taffy Pink" by the same company.

Another choice, if you have only a few blocks in one pattern, and some of another, is to combine the two, as in the Blue Baby quilt on page 39. Even a thirties' sampler quilt might be a good choice to use a varied collection of quilt blocks. Care must be taken when combining blocks, to use only those blocks that will go well together, or to pull it all together with a graphic setting.

If your five blocks just won't work into a quilt, consider making five pillows to give your family as Christmas gifts, or five framed blocks for country decorating, especially if these were made by a member of the family.

Illustration from the Montgomery Ward 1933 catalog used with permission of Montgomery Ward & Co., p. 19.

CHARACTERISTICS OF THIRTIES' QUILTS

Most of the quilts made between the wars were made in the decade of the thirties, but by no means all. Many quilts were made in the twenties. Some of these were traditional patterns, perhaps pieced from turn-of-the-century fabric. But by the late twenties, pastels were popular and experimental patterns were common. Also, if a person made a quilt in 1942 from fabrics and a pattern saved from 1935, it would be considered a thirties' period quilt. So, although a thirties' quilt generally was made in the 1930s, other quilts can fit into this classification.

Thirties' quilts tend to be "homey." Dare I say that the ladies had begun to lose some of their hand-sewing skills? The sewing machine was in general use, and people had been buying clothes by mail order or from department stores since the turn of the century. In thirties' quilts you are less likely to find twenty stitches to the inch and more likely to find a tied quilt. On the other hand, quilts of this period often were made from unusual patterns. These women were willing to try new things. Quilting was changing from a folk art, where methods are handed down from mother to daughter, patterns are preserved in the family, and technique is perfected, to contemporary art, where everyone wants to learn from an expert teacher or a book, where the excitement is often in experimentation, and where the artist strives to make a more original statement, a unique piece of beauty.

But quilts were still being made in the traditions of the past. Not everyone made a "different" quilt. Not everyone had forgotten how to hand-sew, either. Ladies still made some quilts in blue and white or red and white, in the old patterns, and in solid-color fabrics.

Fabric

A number of characteristics set thirties' quilts apart from earlier work and make them different from quilts of a later period. The first difference you'll probably notice is the appearance of the fabrics. (Oh how I love them!) Various advances in fabric manufacturing were made, so that by the twenties, a wide range of colors was available, and almost any pattern could be printed. A wild profusion of colors and patterns became available, yet all showed certain characteristics. Fabrics of the twenties still had a Victorian delicacy of design, precision of engraving, tendency towards naturalism or fantasy, and often a sentimental subject. The Art Noveau movement

was an influence on textile art of the twenties.

As the 1920s progressed, other influences began to appear in fabric design. Art movements like cubism and surrealism were catching the imagination of designers. Also, new admiration for machines and technology was expressed in many ways, including fabric. As the depression began to affect everyone, manufacturers cut cost by lowering the thread count of fabric. Many patterns were printed in one color on white, or white space was left around each color, so no care needed to be taken with registration.

Fabric patterns with thirties' characteristics.

Printed batiste and sateen became fashionable. One lady remembers being glad when she could get some decent material instead of "that crummy sateen."

For some reason, I find myself drawn to another interesting fabric of the thirties: embossed cotton. Printed or plain fabric was pressed between shaped rollers, making a raised pattern in the fabric. Washing or water-spotting tended to remove this raised pattern, but some pieces that I have washed and ironed still show the relief to some extent.

All of these are characteristic of a thirties' quilt top: repeat geometrics, weird clowns and bunnies, pattern after pattern next to each other. Fabrics in one quilt top may include sateen, feedsack in a printed pattern, unbleached muslin, printed gauze, and high-quality percale. Women did not hesitate to use the fabrics at hand and mix them freely.

Color

Color is the second outstanding characteristic of thirties' quilts. Particular colors show up in every other quilt top of the period. One of these was "thirties green." People who are familiar with old quilts know exactly what it looks like.

Many of the colors of this period are pastels or softened colors. Most common among these are "thirties' green," pink, lavender, a buttery yellow, a light blue or blue-green, and soft brown or tan. Popular solids also included a strong burgundy; a bright, clear red; and a bright, clear blue. These colors also were used over and over in prints, in combination, or as one color on white. In the twenties and forties, color preferences were also evident. Pastels were the "in" colors in the twenties, while brighter colors became favorites of the forties.

Fabric patterns with twenties' characteristics.

Typical thirties' pastel colors are used in this appliqued pansy block.

Solid colors found on a swatch book page from the thirties.

Favorite Patterns

Outstanding among common quilt patterns at this time were some very familiar types of quilts. Dresden Plate was a popular pattern. Fan patterns were pieced with many variations. Then there was the Double Wedding Ring, one of the most popular patterns for both quilts and unquilted tops. A needlework column, most likely taken from the *Wisconsin News* about 1932, reads "Please publish . . . The Double Wedding Ring quilt pattern and a suitable quilting design for it . . . during the past few weeks, so many letters carried this request . . . there are fads in quilting . . . and at the present time the Double Wedding Ring is one of the most widely known patterns . . . "

Another very popular pattern was Sunbonnet Sue. "Kate Greenaway, whose illustrations in children's books were so popular worldwide from 1885 into the early 1900's,"[4] was probably the original inspiration for the Sunbonnet Sue patterns, but by the twenties, Sue had begun to show her face everywhere, in both embroidered and applique quilts. Her dresses often were made from scraps left after making everyday dresses, bloomers, and aprons.

After the newspapers had exhausted everyone's collection of old patterns, they started publishing variations, original patterns, and variations of original patterns, whatever they could find. Some of these were almost unworkable and some were exciting. Quilters across the country

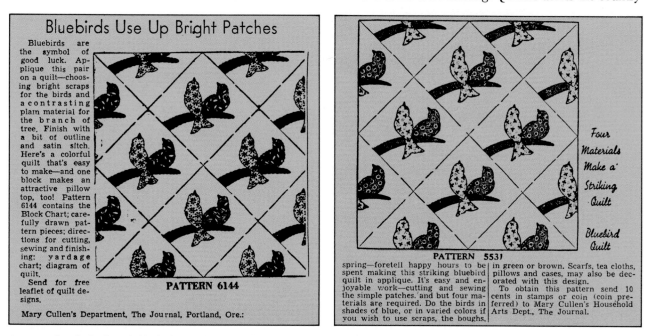

Bluebirds Use Up Bright Patches

Bluebirds are the symbol of good luck. Applique this pair on a quilt—choosing bright scraps for the birds and a contrasting plain material for the branch of tree. Finish with a bit of outline and satin stitch. Here's a colorful quilt that's easy to make—and one block makes an attractive pillow top, too! Pattern 6144 contains the Block Chart; carefully drawn pattern pieces; directions for cutting, sewing and finishing; yardage chart; diagram of quilt.

Send for free leaflet of quilt designs.

Mary Cullen's Department, The Journal, Portland, Ore.:

PATTERN 6144

Four Materials Make a Striking Quilt

Bluebird Quilt

PATTERN 5531

spring—foretell happy hours to be spent making this striking bluebird quilt in applique. It's easy and enjoyable work—cutting and sewing the simple patches, and but four materials are required. Do the birds in shades of blue, or in varied colors if you wish to use scraps, the boughs, in green or brown. Scarfs, tea cloths, pillows and cases, may also be decorated with this design.

To obtain this pattern send 10 cents in stamps or coin (coin preferred) to Mary Cullen's Household Arts Dept., The Journal.

Compare the Bluebirds quilt blocks featured twice in the same newspaper. Different texts, different fabric prints, different pattern numbers, and definitely different prices were used for each.

Newspaper clippings and a pattern from the thirties.

A thirties' variation of Sunbonnet Sue.

cut these out of the newspapers. Judging by dates available, many newspapers published one quilt pattern a week for at least ten years—a total of 520 different quilt patterns. These illustrations almost invariably showed four to nine blocks set together edge to edge, without other blocks of plain fabric or setting strips. Many prints and muslin would be suggested to piece the block illustrated.

Quilt kits were available in the thirties. "One could order stamped or basted tops or hot iron transfers from The Anne Orr Studio."[5] Ruby McKim Studios in Missouri was the "mail-order outlet for their needlework items."[6] Other ladies throughout the country had their own cottage industries selling patterns and kits by mail order.

Many of these kits were children's quilts—crib or youth size. New to the twentieth century was the recognition of children as special, soft human beings with different interests than adults. So the theme of these quilts might be a series of nursery rhymes or animal illustrations, appliqued in soft colors, embroidered, or done in pieced pictures of original design.

As you become familiar with fabric, colors, and patterns in old quilts, the characteristics of thirties' quilts will identify them as "one-of-a-kind."

MARGARET MARONEK

My mother, Margaret Mary Waldkirch Maronek (Marge), was born on a farm in Russel, Illinois on November 6, 1909. Her father, a plumber, sold his business when my mother was four, and the family moved to Saukville, Wisconsin, near Milwaukee. A year later, the family moved into their new home on an eighty-acre dairy farm in Brown Deer, Wisconsin. The house was built of warm yellow brick, with four bedrooms upstairs and four rooms down. There was a wood stove for cooking and heating and a coal stove in the living room. There was no running water, no toilets, no electricity.

There were four boys and four girls in the family. One of the boys died of pneumonia at fourteen. Every day, one of the girls helped with the housework. The others had farm work just like the men. The family grew crops to feed the animals in winter—corn, hay, potatoes, and cabbage.

Waldkirch is a German name that means "church in the woods," and the family ate good German food. They made their own blood sausage, liver sausage, and summer sausage. They rendered lard on the wood stove and baked bread on it, and they made sauerkraut.

On Saturdays my Grandma Waldkirch made kuchen (coffee cake) and pies. Regular meals consisted of one or two vegetables, potatoes, meat, and pickles—maybe pickled crab apples, cucumbers, or pickled beets. The family made their own butter and cottage cheese. If the cottage cheese wasn't eaten fresh, it was heated with caraway seeds and eaten as "cooked cheese." My mother says it smelled terrible. This was spread on bread, like jelly. A lot of food was put by in the basement since it was cool there.

Every day they milked fifteen to twenty cows, morning and evening. They always had two to four horses, since they plowed, cultivated, planted, and harvested by horsepower. Jobs for the children included picking stones out of the fields, when they were plowed and planted, and pulling the mustard weed out of the grain, when the grain was twelve inches high.

My mother fed the chickens and minded the cows while they were at pasture or grazing along the road. Her special job was picking the cherry trees. Some cherries were canned, some were made immediately into pies, and the excess was made into cherry wine.

My father grew up across the river from my mother's family and was a friend of her older brother. On their first date he took her to the museum and her older broth-

Butterfly, by Margaret Maronek, Milwaukee, Wisconsin, 1935, 62″ x 78″. Tattered and faded, this quilt still has something to teach about thirties' patterns, colors, and fabrics. (Collection of Sara Nephew)

ers made fun of them.

My mother became interested in quilting after she was engaged to be married. She needed covers for their twin beds, and two quilts were cheaper to make than the price of two bedspreads. Also, quilting seemed like it would be a fun thing to do.

Her sister's mother-in-law had made a Butterfly quilt. It was talked up so much in the family that they asked her to send it from Nebraska to a large department store in Milwaukee, so it could be displayed in a quilt contest. (Stores promoted quilting to sell fabric.) Marge liked the quilt, too, and decided to make two Butterfly quilts as part of her trousseau. They were a labor of love. She planned the allover design with borders herself and bought new fabric for the quilts. She didn't like the square wings on the butterflies of the original design, so she rounded them off. When the tops were finished, she quilted them. She didn't mark the top for quilting but held up a cardboard strip to continually measure as she quilted the grid.

Margaret Waldkirch and Arthur Maronek, my parents, on their wedding day (1935). My father is standing directly behind my mother.

When my parents were married in 1935, the economy was improving. They bought a house from a mortgage foreclosure and lived upstairs, while they rented the downstairs flat. The upstairs was unfinished and was just one big open space. The only partition was around the bathroom, which was also unfinished. For their first Christmas, they bought each other a bathtub with twenty dollars they had borrowed.

My mother worked as a secretary for six years after her marriage. I was born eighteen days after the attack on Pearl Harbor. My brother was born a year and a half later. During the war, my father worked as a machinist thirteen hours a day, seven days a week, and my mother took care of almost everything else. In 1946 our family was increased by three, when my younger sisters (triplets) were born. My mother didn't do handwork, except for darning socks, for a long, long time. She kept four sacks of quilting fabric in her closet, but I remember her hoeing in the garden, freezing and canning vegetables and fruits, or butchering chickens. When it wasn't summer or fall, she sewed clothes for us children.

My mother makes some quilts now for the grandchildren. A few years ago, she sent me the two quilts with ap-

pliqued butterflies. One was almost in pieces, so I framed portions of it as Christmas gifts for my brother and sisters. The other quilt, though tattered, is in my collection.

CLARA MCNIGHT HULL

Dolores Wagner, of Snohomish, Washington, inherited a number of thirties' quilts and tops from her mother and her mother's aunt. Dolores' mother, Clara McNight Hull, was born in Milton, Tennessee. She was educated as a school teacher and taught on the Flathead Indian Reservation in Pablo, Montana for 15 years, until her marriage. Clara lived in a rooming house there with other ladies and school teachers, and they made quilts together.

Dolores picked up quilting on her own, having never been formally taught. However, her grandmother and her mother did a lot of needlework. She threaded needles for her grandma and was allowed to try out a treadle machine, but not sew with it. She remembers making a homemade loom, and as a young girl, she sewed and designed doll clothes. She was also taught to knit.

During the summer her Grandma and Grandpa Mc-

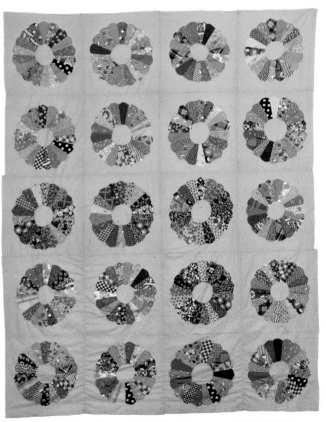

Dresden Plate, by Clara Hull, Pablo, Montana, c. 1930, 70½″ x 90″. A popular pattern from the thirties is bright when made with scraps on golden yellow. Many fabric designs were available, even though money was hard to come by. (Collection of Dolores Wagner)

Clara Hull (c. 1930).

and did much of her quilting there. At home she was the force behind most quiltmaking. When she and her three sisters decided on a design, they would cut and piece four quilt tops in that design, one for each of them. Frankie married and had four children: three daughters and a son, who died young.

Frankie and her sisters made many quilt tops, quilts, and summer quilts. Diane remembers lying on the bed under many a summer quilt and seeing the sunlight filtering through the top, the fabric and color making designs like a kaleidoscope.

Frankie was a fabricaholic. When Diane's parents moved to California for a while, Grandma Frankie sent them bolts of fabric and brought them more when she visited.

Diane has fond memories of her grandmother and grandfather, and of her great aunts and those times. Diane remembers the colorful fabrics in her great aunt's aprons, many of which were made from printed flour sacks that the flour came in. Her grandfather and her uncle would take her along to the tavern every afternoon at 4:00 and buy her an ice cream. Sometimes it would be a Babe Ruth candy bar for two cents.

Diane's grandmother and her great aunts left many

Night would let Dolores and her brother and sister stay in their four-room farm house. The only electricity came from eight to twelve big acid batteries in an outbuilding. This provided light for milking the cows. Light in the house would be turned on at 6:00 p.m. and off at 9:30, when everyone went to bed. Dolores and her sister slept between two fat feather beds, like a sandwich. On top of each sandwich bed was a heavy, tied quilt made from big wool blocks.

There was no hot water, so on Saturday night they would build up the fire and heat a big tub of water. The three children would then take a bath, one after the other. By the time the last one got in, the water would be cold.

FRANCES MISSOULA
PETHOUD PHILLIPS

Frances Missoula Pethoud was born in Missoula, Montana, one of thirteen children. Her granddaughter, Diane Coombs, inherited a number of her quilt tops. Frances taught Diane to embroider, though Diane was only five when her grandmother died. Frances had a strong personality and was always a very stylish person. She was voted best-dressed in high school.

They called her Frankie. She worked the graveyard shift of the CB & Q railroad as a switchboard operator

Frances Missoula Pethoud Phillips and William Edward Phillips, c. 1930.

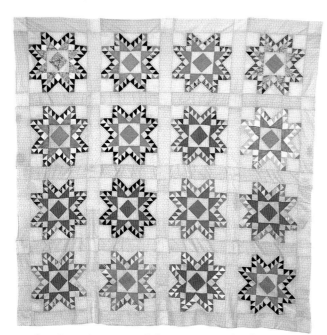

Feathered Star, by Frances Phillips, Beatrice, Nebraska, c. 1925, 89″ x 91″. Although the fabrics in this quilt are from the twenties, some characteristic thirties' colors are already evident. It's exciting to see how different the Feathered Star patterns look when the dark and light values of the little feathers are reversed. (Collection of Diane Coombs)

unfinished tops and were great savers of fabric, so Diane feels that she came by these characteristics in herself quite honestly.

Marina and John Perecz on the afternoon of their wedding day in 1936, as they were leaving for their honeymoon.

MARINA PERECZ

Marina Esser Perecz was originally from northern Minnesota. In 1930, when she was fifteen, her whole family came to Washington State in an old truck and settled near Snohomish.

Marina was never taught to quilt, but her family had quilts for daily use, and she learned sewing, knitting, and crocheting by being around others who did handwork and by teaching herself. She says it's really so easy now, with all the books telling how to do things. Although piecing and quilting are easy, she says, "You don't need fancy stuff, just plain commonsense arithmetic."

Before her marriage in 1936, Marina embroidered the blocks for a State Flowers quilt. The patterns for this quilt were printed in the *Seattle Star* in the early thirties. Marina's sister made the same quilt. They used to wait each week for the paper to come with the pattern in it. First, they would trace the pattern actual size onto "store paper" (heavy white paper used to wrap packages). Then, they pierced holes along all the lines, using a sew-

State Flowers, (detail) by Marina Perecz, Snohomish, Washington, c. 1930, 77″ x 90″. These Ruby McKim patterns were printed in many newspapers in the thirties. (Collection of Marina Perecz)

ing machine without thread, or, if it was a difficult part of the design, they pierced the holes by hand with a needle. The pierced paper was then laid over fabric. After soaking a rag in cleaning solvent, they rubbed it first over a cake of blue wax, then over the needle-punched paper. The blue liquid went through the holes and left the dotted pattern on the fabric, a guide for embroidery. (This method of marking fabric is no longer recommended.) For her State Flowers quilt, Marina used 80-square tan percale.

When Marina married John Perecz in June of 1936, her grandmother gave her a quilt and feather pillows for a wedding present. The quilt is made from pre-1930 fabrics, although some material could be late twenties. The quilt has a wool batt and is all hand-quilted. Marina has used it carefully and kept it in good condition.

Marina made other quilts, some of which she has given to each of her three children. Most of her designs came from magazines. Except for the backing, she seldom bought new fabric for her quilts. Another embroidered quilt she made was backed with fabric printed in the Wedding Ring design. The quilt border was also printed on this fabric. The border was cut off the central panel of the quilt back, and the pattern matched, so that the back looks like a pieced quilt, unless examined closely. She followed the Wedding Ring pattern on the back when she did the quilting.

GRACE KOENIG

Grace Koenig's parents came to Washington Territory from eastern Canada in 1887. Grace was born in 1895, in the small mill town of McMurray, Washington. The main street of McMurray was two blocks long and consisted of as many saloons (and brothels) as the population could support; a general store, owned and operated by the lumber company; a post office; a meat market; a barber shop; and another general grocery with the town's meeting room on the second floor. The town was across a small lake from her home. Her mother could always see what her children were doing by simply looking out the window.

Grace remembers her father being worried about jobs and money during the "depression." But this depression was a financial downturn in the early 1900s following the Spanish-American War.

Grace's father worked twelve hours a day, seven days a week, for a dollar a day. In three years he was able to save forty dollars, and he used the money to buy a cow. This was the first of a small dairy herd, which furnished

Grace Koenig and her child (1912).

Grandmother's Flower Garden, by Grace Koenig, Mt. Vernon, Washington, c. 1935, 77½" x 94". Pieced with tiny diamond stepping-stones between the flower bouquets, this hexagon pattern was a favorite in the thirties, and still is. (Collection of Donna Prentice)

the whole town with milk.

No one taught Grace how to piece or quilt, but quilts were always around to use as bedcovers and were made from scraps. In the late 1920s, Grace suffered a severe nervous breakdown, which confined her to a wheelchair or required her to use a cane for over seven years. She needed something to do with her hands. She got hold of a roll of cotton (a quilt batt) and found the pattern for a Dresden Plate quilt rolled up inside. This was the first quilt she made.

She pieced the quilt from fabric she found in a piece bag, a 100-lb. flour sack containing every scrap saved from home sewing, and used home-carded wool for the batt. She quilted it beautifully and later won first prize at the Western Washington State Fair in Puyallup. This quilt is now the property of Grace's grandson.

Grace made two lavender Double Wedding Ring quilts. She asked all of her relatives and friends in the United States and Canada to send her two-inch strips of every orchid print they could find. Finally, duplicates began coming in, and she called a halt to the collecting. Grace used some of the fabrics left over from the first Wedding Ring quilt in another quilt, pictured on page 38, that features the conventional violet, her favorite flower.

Grace has made many quilts. The Poppy Quilt on page 41 was made during the thirties. She saw the picture of the quilt in a library book and wrote to the author, who had a small quilt shop in Wisconsin. Grace could have purchased the quilt as a kit, but instead bought only the pattern from her. During the 1970s, Grace taught classes in piecing and quilting.

LOTTIE RANSDELL

Lottie Ransdell was born November 16, 1903, in Mercer County, Kentucky. She grew up on a farm, one of nine children. Her family was very close and had a lot of happy times on the farm. Social life revolved around the church. Quilts and making quilts were a familiar part of everyday life.

Lottie married a young man who had grown up in the same area. She and her husband had five children, three of whom are still living. She remained a housewife until World War II, when she went to work in a parachute factory. The family moved to Lexington, Kentucky in 1935 and to Indiana in 1945, where Lottie still lives.

Lottie still makes quilts, some of which she sells. One of her customers was a doctor, who would buy about twelve quilts a year. She is eighty-four now and her eyes

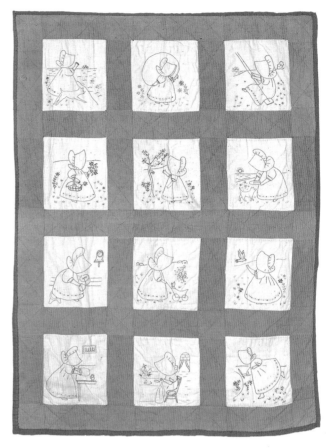

Sunbonnet Sue, by Lottie Ransdell, Kentucky, c. 1930, 33″ x 43″. These little embroidered girls in their prairie bonnets look like some of the earliest drawings of Sunbonnet Sue. (Collection of Mary Meyer)

Lottie and Lee Ransdell (c. 1940).

are failing, but she still quilts for others.

All of her quilts are hand-pieced and hand-quilted. Quilts for her own use were made mostly from clothing scraps and feed sacks. After the top is pieced, Lottie bastes the layers together on the floor with straight pins every eight to ten inches. She used to keep a frame set up in her room, but now she uses big hoops.

Her daughter, Mary Meyer, for whom the embroidered quilt was made, wasn't interested in learning to make quilts as a child, but says she "picked up enough information to be dangerous," and is now interested in quilting. On a recent visit to her daughter's home, Lottie saw a quilt top Mary had made. Lottie took it home, and in three weeks, mailed it back, quilted. It was "a good double—a little shy of queen size."

ELNORA GREGG MARSH

Elnora Gregg was born in 1868 in Kansas. She grew up on a farm and married a traveling blacksmith named Leonardo Marsh. His circuit covered Kansas, Missouri, and Nebraska. Elnora learned to make quilts as a normal part of her life. She was always a homemaker.

In the 1920s and 1930s she lived with her son, Morti-

Elnora Marsh with her son, Jess Marsh (November 1955).

mer, and his family in Hastings, Nebraska. There, she began a quilt made from sixty-degree diamonds. This family had three girls and each got two new dresses each summer. The center of the quilt is pieced from the scraps of these dresses.

Then Elnora moved in with another relative in Scotts Bluff, Nebraska. The piecing of the quilt continued there, with all the outside pieces being added from this new family's collection of scraps.

This quilt was given to her youngest granddaughter, Mildred Marsh, as a wedding present about 1943. Eventually, it was given to Marsha McCloskey, a Seattle quilt author and teacher, by her mother. Marsha did not get to know her great-grandmother very well, but she remembers meeting her once when Marsha was nine or ten and Elnora was a tiny white-haired woman of ninety-three. She was ill in bed at the time. She had fallen and broken her hip while washing her feet in the sink.

HENRIETTA MOORE MICHAEL

Born October 19, 1856, Henrietta Moore came from Missouri to southern Indiana in a covered wagon. She married a coal miner, Gideon Michael, and they had nine children.

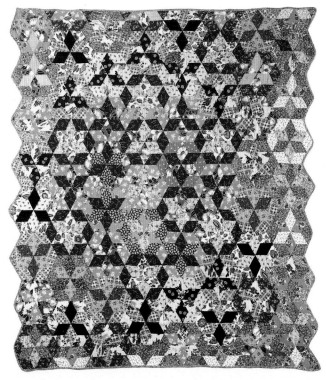

Hexagon Stars, by Elnora Marsh, Hastings, Nebraska, c. 1930, 70" x 82". The arrangement of dark and light values in this quilt produces striking graphics. (Collection of Marsha McCloskey)

Crystal Honeycomb, by Henrietta Michael, Jasonville, Indiana, c. 1930, 84″ x 91½″. The unusual design and the mix of textures and colors in this quilt top make it an outstanding example of the period. (Collection of Pamela Foster)

Four generations of quilters, clockwise, beginning at top left: Henrietta Michael, Helen Rasner Eder, Mae Michael Rasner, Debbie Eder Payne, and Pamela Eder Foster.

Henrietta eventually came to live with her youngest child, Mae. Henrietta and Mae made quilts together, and Mae's daughter, Helen, cut pieces for their quilts. Henrietta sewed for others and kept the scraps. She also did quilting for other people and used the money to buy new fabric. She pieced by hand until well into her eighties, when her eyesight began to fail. Mae also pieced quilts. Helen can tell you now who pieced which quilt top, because red was her mother's favorite color.

Henrietta and Mae used new material for their quilt tops and copied patterns from the newspapers. In the thirties, they paid nineteen cents per yard for good cotton and fifteen cents a yard for cheaper cottons. They always bought the best fabrics they could afford, much of it from J. C. Penney. The two ladies regularly got together with their missionary society for a quilting bee. The men threw horseshoes and the women quilted.

Henrietta died in August 1965. After Mae died, her granddaughter, Pamela Foster, inherited many of her quilt tops, which she intends to quilt.

MARGARET WESSEL ZANON

Margaret Wessel was born in Halle, Germany on June 8, 1906. She came to Galveston, Texas with her mother, when she was three years old. At five years of age, she moved with her mother and stepfather to Madrid, New Mexico, where her stepfather worked as a coal miner. She had many Spanish-American neighbors and learned to love hot, spicy foods. Her mother worked in other people's homes, cleaning and doing laundry, and Margaret helped with chores at home. When she was eight or nine, she remembers bringing a horse into the kitchen "just to see what it would look like." She was helped in this experiment by neighbor children, and evidently one of them didn't know how to keep a secret, as her mother found out from a neighbor.

Besides working outside the home, her mother took in boarders. Margaret had to help cook and do the dishes, especially when her mother was pregnant. (Margaret has two sisters and a brother.) All water had to be carried to the house in a bucket from a distance of about a block.

The Spanish flu epidemic in 1918 killed many, and, at that time, the coal mines in New Mexico shut down. The family decided to move to Red Lodge, Montana in 1919. When Margaret was eighteen, she met Martin Zanon, who came to Red Lodge to work in the coal mines. She was nineteen when she married him, in September of 1925.

In April of 1926, Margaret and Martin headed for

Trip Around the World, by Margaret Zanon, Snohomish, Washington, 1939, 82" x 86". This quilt was started with three squares in the middle, so that when it was finished, it would have a rectangular rather than a square shape. Done primarily in solid colors, this quilt presents an interesting collection of thirties' pastels. (A gift from Margaret Zanon to the author's collection)

Margaret and Martin Zanon's wedding picture (1925). She was nineteen.

Clearview, Washington in a Hupmobile. It took them a whole week to get through the mountains of Idaho and Washington. They had no lights, so they could not travel at night.

They lived, at first, in a small cabin with a door on each end and two windows. There was a wood stove and kerosene lamps. Martin's two brothers, who had come to Clearview earlier, moved into the little shed out back. The landscape consisted of giant stumps and low brush, because the area had been logged off a few years before. Margaret picked wild blackberries in the brush.

The couple added rooms, gradually making a large house out of the cabin. The stumps were cleared and strawberries were planted. Martin had jobs building roads and working in the shipyards, but during the summer he was a strawberry farmer.

Margaret took in laundry, cared for and milked the family cow, kept 200 chickens, canned 800-900 quarts of food a year, and had three children. She had never made a quilt until one of her neighbors helped her make a Dutch Doll quilt. Another neighbor gave her a few squares and some fabric and helped her start a Trip Around the World quilt. This quilt was made mostly from scraps, but some fabric had to be purchased. Margaret's younger sister, Ruth, who was about sixteen, also worked on the quilt. They finished it in 1939. Shortly afterwards, Ruth contracted tuberculosis, and Margaret nursed her for a year in an upstairs bedroom of her home until she recovered.

Margaret Zanon has continued to make quilts, giving them to her children and grandchildren. She also makes a baby quilt for each child born in her church.

NELLIE HARRIS ROSS

Nellie Harris Ross, 1874-1957, was raised in Iowa on a farm. She married and had thirteen children. The family traveled a lot. Once, when they were living on a houseboat in Arkansas, one of her daughters died of malaria. Nellie's husband was a Civil War veteran (having managed to enlist at the age of twelve or fourteen) and was quite a bit older than she was. When he died, she went to apply for a pension as a Civil War widow. She found that she was not eligible, since her husband had been married before and had never bothered to get a divorce.

Nellie made and gave many quilts to her children.

Double Wedding Ring, by Nellie Ross, c. 1930, origin unknown, 69″ x 82″. Bright colors and strongly patterned fabrics make this quilt a lot of fun. (Collection of Molly Barry)

Molly Barry, Nellie's great-granddaughter, inherited this Double Wedding Ring as a top. She made some small repairs, then quilted and bound it, completing the quilt in 1987.

MARY SMITH

Mary Smith, 1873-1957, was born and grew up in Minnesota. Her family farmed for part of every year and spent the rest of the time working in Duluth. Mary learned to quilt as a matter of course, since every family she knew had quilts.

She was married to a man named Higgens first, and had two children, a boy and a girl. Her husband died and she married Charlie Mills. They had another girl. Mary and Mr. Mills separated in 1918. In the 1920's she married a Mr. McLaughlin. Later at the age of 80, she married Mr. Smith. Her fourth husband only lived six months. Later she was teased that she "wore him out" (which adds to the evidence that quilters are a long-lived group).

Mary made many quilts in her lifetime. Her children and grandchildren were all given quilts, and she taught

Nellie Ross at 56 (1928).

Tulip Basket, by Mary Smith, Bellingham, Washington, c. 1940, 82″ x 93″. This quilt was started from a kit in 1938 and completed in 1986. It combines a sparkling and unusual design, beautiful applique and embroidery, and thirties' colors. It is a superior example of the period. (Collection of Edward and Sylvia McFadden)

Mary Smith and her daughter, Gertrude (1918 or 1919).

spending her life taking care of her younger brother and sisters, "married her off" to a friend of his. The marriage was not a success. The couple lived in a log house, which had lost its chinking, and when her husband caught her looking out through the cracks, he would complain that she wanted to look at the younger people. He said he wanted to "keep her like a pet." She went back home to her father and got a divorce.

In all, Lillie Mae was married four times. Her second husband was a coal miner, and the small family lived in a sod dugout. One morning, when Lillie woke, she saw a snake in the bed between her and the baby. Lillie jumped out of bed and grabbed a pitchfork to throw the snake away from the baby. As soon as she poked the snake, it wrapped itself around the pitchfork, but she somehow managed to kill it.

Lillie's third marriage was difficult, and in 1916, in order to support her family, she had to leave and take a job as a matron in a boys' orphanage. Her children were cared for by her sister and her oldest daughter, Ava, who was by then married with young children of her own.

Lillie Mae had eight children, five girls and three boys. One boy died of pheumonia, one died in a motorcy-

her daughters to quilt. The beautiful Tulip Basket quilt was a quilt kit. It was started in 1938 and finished only recently. Sylvia McFadden, the wife of Mary's grandson and an accomplished quilter, did some additional applique and embroidery (the unfinished pieces had been basted in place). Then Sylvia quilted it, completing the quilt in 1986.

LILLIE MAE HEDRICK ROMINE

Lillie Mae Hedrick was born July 7, 1875, in Gol County, Illinois. She had three sisters and one brother. Her father worked for the railroad, and the family lived in a little shanty, which was moved along as the railroad was built. Eventually, the family arrived in Oklahoma, when it was still Indian Territory.

Her mother died when Lillie was fourteen years old. Her father, concerned that she would be trapped into

Bars, by Lillie Romine, c. 1925, origin unknown, 65 1/2″ x 77½″. This quilt was pieced from various silklike fabrics and then tied. The maker's good sense of color and design make this more than just a scrap quilt. Lillie's grandchildren always wanted to sleep under this quilt. (Collection of John and Dana Graupmann)

Lillie Mae Romine (c. 1948).

August 4, 1852. She was married to Lewis Lillard Shelley on January 20, 1869. They journeyed by covered wagon to Missouri and then to Kansas. The family grew to nine boys and four girls. In 1902 the family came to Oregon by train. One story handed down indicates they intended to go to Klamath Falls, but the railroad only went as far as Ashland, and they heard Klamath Falls was overrun with water snakes. "The many snakes lay in balls under the board sidewalks and as one walked down the street, the snake heads sticking up through the cracks between the boards were like ten pins." The family decided to settle in Ashland.

Continuing to pursue a better life, the family moved to Little Shasta Valley, Siskiyou County, California in 1914. Many members of the family still live in this area.

The Shelleys owned a general merchandise store in many of the places they lived. So, the women of the family always had new material for quilts. Their friends thought they were weird for cutting up new fabric.

All of the girls helped make quilts. Even later, when everyone had married and some had moved away, family

cle accident, and the third one, after being gassed in World War II, died of tuberculosis.

Lillie always quilted with church groups or Ladies' Aid. She took quilts to families who needed bedcovers. She felt that quilts were made from necessity and that everything could be made into a quilt. Between 1910 and 1912, she made a living, sewing clothes for a judge, who was a big man and couldn't find shirts to fit him. She refused to teach her children to sew because she felt they couldn't do it right, but the girls all later became accomplished seamstresses.

A quilt Lillie made from ties and other silklike scraps is now owned by her great-granddaughter, Dana Graupmann. Dana remembers all the children wanting to sleep under this quilt, whenever they were ill.

MELISSA HEALEN SNOW SHELLEY

Melissa Healen Snow was born in Kentucky on

Melissa Shelley with two of her children (c. 1900).

French Bouquet, by Melissa Shelley, Siskiyou County, California, c. 1935, 77″ x 92″. Block placement suggests this quilt was planned for a bed against the wall. An especially pleasing combination of lavender shades, as well as other pastels and prints, makes this top a welcome addition to any collection. (Collection of John and Dana Graupmann)

visits, holidays, and reunions were spent all together around the quilting frame.

Melissa quilted until she could no longer see well, and someone else had to thread needles for her. These quilt tops now belong to Dana and John Graupmann, Melissa's great-grandson. Dana intends to quilt the tops some day.

GALLERY OF QUILTS

Crazy Patch, origin unknown, c. 1930, 74″ x 86″. This quilt was completely assembled from scraps of pique, a lightly ribbed weave. The color selection is certainly thirties'. (A gift from Nina Nicholl to the author's collection)

Bias Butterfly, by Sara Nephew, 1987, Snohomish, Washington, 52″ x 67½″. This quilt was made in the spirit of the depression, when necessity was the mother of invention. Adding the strips of bias tape to an unfinished collection of old applique blocks turned them into a new design with radiant pastels. (Collection of the author) (Pattern on page 55)

Fan Doll Quilt, by Sara Nephew, 1983, Snohomish, Washington, 25″ x 29″. The fans in this quilt were cut from a set of partially pieced "dandelions." (Collection of the author) (Pattern on page 63)

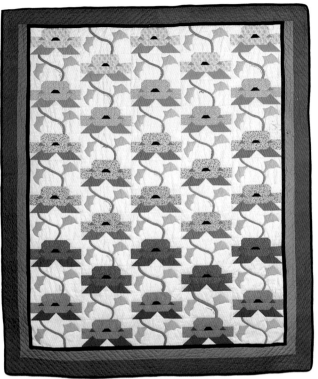

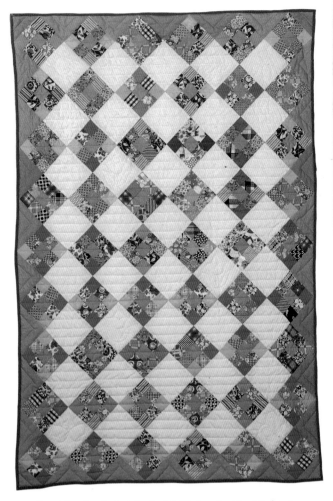

Oriental Poppy, by the Busy Bee Quilters of Snohomish, Washington, 1985, 80″ x 90″. This design was published by Ruby McKim in 1931. Mar Tobiason interpreted it in modern solid-color fabrics of increasing intensity, for a result both delicate and effective. (Collection of Mar Tobiason, Everett, Washington)

Random Nine-Patch, by Marsha McCloskey, Seattle, Washington, 1987, 39½″ x 58″. The soft colors and simple geometry of this small quilt give it an art-deco feel. (Collection of Marsha McCloskey)

Star-Spangled Banner, by Sara Nephew, Snohomish, Washington, 1987, 48″ x 48″. Any pattern may be given a new flavor by using thirties' pastels. The dark feathers in this top were pieced from a black polka-dot cotton. The star is from the book, "Feathered Star Quilts," by Marsha McCloskey, published by That Patchwork Place in 1987. (Collection of the author)

Nine-Patch, by Mae Rasner, Beech Grove, Indiana, c. 1930, 80½″ x 88″. The tiny size of these nine-patches totally changes the appearance of this familiar design. (Collection of Pamela Foster)

Fan Medallion, by Sara Nephew, Snohomish, Washington, 1984, 43½″ x 43″. In this small quilt, fans and sawtooth borders combine for an art-deco look. This quilt was influenced in both color and form by thirties' design. (Collection of Sara Nephew) (Pattern on page 63)

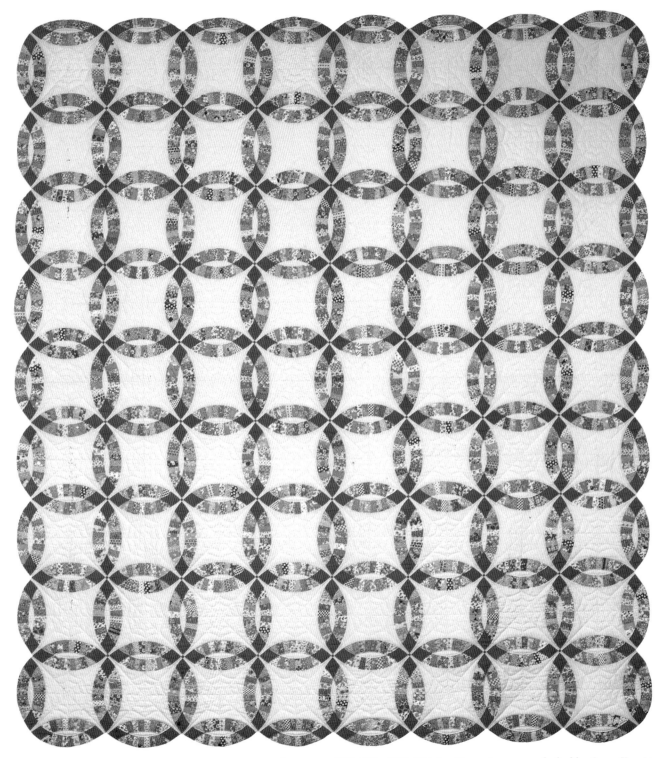

Double Wedding Ring, by Grace Koenig, Mt. Vernon, Washington, c. 1935, 92″ x 103″. This familiar pattern was redrafted by Grace Koenig to make the circles perfectly round. A stylized violet connects the rings. (Collection of Grace Koenig)

Blue Baby Quilt, by Sara Nephew, Snohomish, Washington, 1983, 45″ x 45″. Three Rolling Stone blocks and six Tea Party blocks combined surprisingly well in one small quilt and then were quickly quilted by machine. (Collection of the author) (Patterns on pages 60 and 62)

Three Across, by Sara Nephew, 1987, Snohomish, Washington, 47″ x 57″. This pattern was designed with a pieced butterfly to counteract the vampire butterfly in my mother's thirties' pattern collection. Other arrangements of the square allow a butterfly to be more easily seen. The quilt top was pieced almost exclusively from depression-era fabrics. (Collection of the author) (Pattern on page 50)

Nine-Patch, origin unknown, c. 1930, 73″ x 83″. The color play in this quilt calls to mind the sparkle and shadow of light shining through the leaves of a large tree. (Collection of Sara Nephew)

Sunbonnet Sue, by Rose Herrera, Snohomish, Washington, 1987, 49″ x 61″. A stack of these blocks was purchased at a garage sale. Only one or two were finished, but embroidery designs had been penciled on. These designs are very Victorian (notice the buttoned shoes), although the applique shapes of dress and hat are typical of the thirties. A found fabric supplied the setting strips. (Collection of Rose Herrera)

New Star, origin unknown, c. 1930, 65½″ x 83″. The interesting design of this star was made more exciting by the splashy prints of the thirties. The quilt was finished neatly with prairie points. (Collection of Mary Fox)

Pansy, maker unknown, c. 1930, 84″ x 86″. The pastels in these pansies sometimes show through overlapping fabrics to form new colors. The embroidered detail adds a lot to the pansy's appeal. (Collection of Judy Hodson) (Pattern on page 54)

Applique Poppy, by Grace Koenig, Mt. Vernon, Washington, c. 1935, 84″ x 94″. This wonderful quilt is an excellent example of thirties'
applique. The stitches are so tiny that no petal or flower will ever come loose. Grace made three of these quilts. (Collection of Grace Koenig)

Field of Diamonds, by Ida Gaulke and her mother, Milwaukee, Wisconsin, 1929, 75″ x 77″. This is an unusual variation of the hexagon pattern. The diamond gardens are arranged by color around the center. An old blanket or possibly another quilt has been used as the batting, making this quilt a heavyweight. (Collection of the author)

Dahlia, origin unknown, c. 1930, 64″ x 89″. The flower in this quilt is a pretty one, but it is entirely overshadowed by the geometry and strong color of the setting strips and the scalloped border—a triumph of design! (Collection of Jocelyn Holm)

Log Chain, origin unknown, c. 1930, 60″ x 80½″. This quilt is primarily made from feedsack materials. Unusual colors and splashy prints combine for a strong graphic effect. (Collection of the author.) (Pattern on page 61)

Rolling Stone, by Diane Coombs, Everett, Washington, 1987, 42″ x 42″. Diane floated the soft pastel thirties' fabrics on a dark green modern background with satisfying results. (Collection of Diane Coombs) (Pattern on page 60)

Tea Party, by Laura Reinstatler, Mill Creek, Washington, 48½″ x 48½″. Modern fabrics mix well with antique materials for a light-hearted quilt easy to live with. Laura included the one mistake required by tradition. (Collection of Laura Reinstatler) (Pattern on page 62)

Fly Foot, by Sara Nephew, Snohomish, Washington, 1983, 60″ x 60″. Thirteen blocks found at a garage sale combine with other thirties' fabrics to make a graphic quilt that's nicely balanced between empty space and active squares. (Collection of the author)

Bow Tie, by Sara Nephew, 1984, Snohomish, Washington, 77″ x 94″. The 4″ bow ties are pieced from depression-era fabrics. The cotton satin background is true to the thirties' spirit and makes a large quilt out of a reasonable number of bow ties. Anonymous quilter. (Collection of the author) (Pattern on page 63)

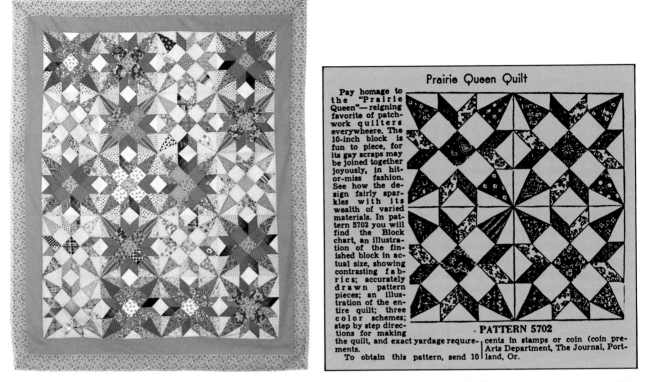

Prairie Queen, by Sara Nephew, 1987, Snohomish, Washington, 51″ x 62″. Starting with seven very pale blocks, stronger colors were added from a collection of thirties' fabrics, making blocks that look like flowers. The result is unique and certainly different from the original newspaper illustration shown here. (Collection of the author) (Pattern on page 57)

Shooting Star, by Christine Russell, Seattle, Washington, 1987, 52″ x 64″. The author redrafted the original pattern from the newspaper column illustrated here to eliminate the narrow, shaded piece on the outside arm. When the blocks are sewn together, eight seams intersect instead of the twelve originally required. Done in scraps on white, this pattern forms an attractive, repeated motion over the surface of the quilt. (Collection of Christine Russell) (Pattern on page 52)

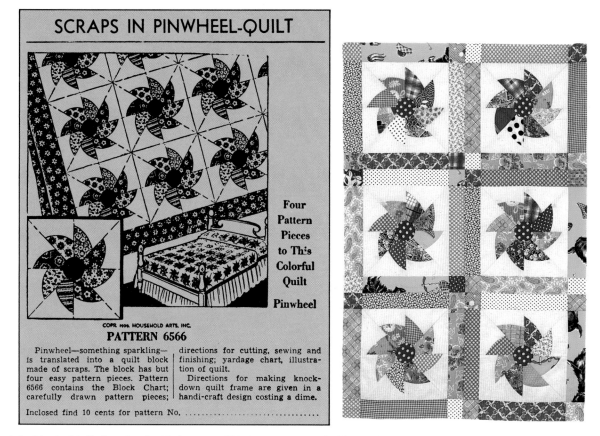

SCRAPS IN PINWHEEL-QUILT

Four Pattern Pieces to This Colorful Quilt

Pinwheel

COPR. 1938 HOUSEHOLD ARTS, INC.

PATTERN 6566

Pinwheel—something sparkling— is translated into a quilt block made of scraps. The block has but four easy pattern pieces. Pattern 6566 contains the Block Chart; carefully drawn pattern pieces;

directions for cutting, sewing and finishing; yardage chart, illustration of quilt.

Directions for making knock-down quilt frame are given in a handi-craft design costing a dime.

Inclosed find 10 cents for pattern No. ....

Pinwheel, by Marsha McCloskey, Seattle, Washington, 1987, 22½″ x 33½″. The blue paisley in this piece is an embossed fabric. Marsha added a frame to the original block from the newspaper clipping shown here to form setting strips. The pattern has a lot of motion and, in this sample, looks like wind-blown daisies. (Collection of Marsha McCloskey) (Pattern on page 53)

Hidden Flower, by Judy Pollard, Seattle, Washington, 1987, 25″ x 36½″. A lively geometric. The curved seam of the original block from the newspaper column shown here was straightened by the author, making the block easier to sew and giving it a more consistent feel. Although Judy was given a limited selection of thirties' prints and plaids to work with, she managed to achieve a warm, scrappy effect. (Collection of Judy Pollard) (Pattern on page 51)

Imperial Fan
Pattern 661

BLOCK IN SCRAPS MAKES LOVELY QUILT

FAN DESIGNS of every variety form handsome blocks and lend themselves to the use of scraps—and what quiltmaker is not pleased at that? Imperial Fan has indeed earned its name, for it has not only all the outstanding features of other Fan blocks, but forms an astonishingly beautiful pattern when the blocks are arranged as shown. In this illustration, only the center formation of the quilt is given. The simple block, shown in greater detail in the enlarged size, is joined to form a flower-like design which grows from the center. This arrangement is very simple to follow. In two quarters of the quilt the blocks all face the same way; in the other two quarters they are reversed. When these are joined the radiating pattern is formed.

Imperial Fan, by Cleo Nollette, Seattle, Washington, 1987, 73″ x 73″. Although the plaids and solids in this quilt are strong, much like those in the newspaper column from the thirties shown on this page, the effect is floral, calling to mind sunflowers and daisies. Thirties' fabrics were combined with modern fabrics. (Collection of Cleo Nollette) (Pattern on page 56)

This Quilt is Colorful In Scraps

Rising Sun

PATTERN 5346

Though many of us have little opportunity nor inclination to see the rising sun, we still find it very lovely to look at in a gay colored quilt. This one, aptly named Rising Sun, will be lovely with the sun's rays made in scraps or in three different materials. The block goes together—before you know it, you'll have enough ready for your quilt.

In pattern 5346 you will find the block chart, an illustration of the finished block in actual size, showing contrasting fabrics; accurately drawn pattern pieces; an illustration of the entire quilt; three color schemes; step-by-step directions for making the quilt, and exact yardage requirements.

To obtain this pattern send 10 cents in stamps or coin (coin preferred) to Mary Cullen's Household Arts Dept., The Journal.

Rising Sun, by Laura Reinstatler, Mill Creek, Washington, 1987, 32″ x 43″. A slight change from the original newspaper clipping shown on this page, so that all points of the rays meet at the curve, simplifies piecing and makes the design stronger. In the spirit of the thirties, a rhyme comes to mind: This small quilt will light the days with many suns and sparkling rays. (Collection of Laura Reinstatler) (Pattern on page 58)

PATTERNS

If you have collected or been given a number of old thirties' quilt patterns or illustrations, you may want to try out some of these patterns. Those printed in the newspapers often had wonderful and encouraging words, telling how much fun they were to do, how proud anyone would be of the results, and how economically they used scraps. Just remember, some of these were never finished for a reason. A bit of analysis is often helpful at first. Consider:

1. Is it easy to do? Many thirties' patterns must be hand-pieced or redrafted for machine sewing. (It almost seems as if some of the designers had never pieced a quilt themselves.) The designers were often trying to produce something new and different, and drawing it was the most important thing. Evaluate the pattern for ease of piecing.
2. Check design qualities. Are there a lot of points, angles, or odd shapes that will detract from the beauty of the design? Does combining the squares produce attractive secondary designs? If it's applique or a pictorial square, the underlying shapes should bring out the meaning of the drawn figure. For example, you could have an applique rose with the underlying shape of a lumpy snail. Analyze the square to see if the results will justify your efforts.

Of course, you may already be attracted by some familiar thirties' patterns and want to try them first. Many of these more common patterns are available, so no drafting is necessary. Sunbonnet Sue, Butterfly, Indian Hatchet, Wedding Ring, and Dresden Plate are all in many pattern books.

Other patterns may only be available to you if drafted from an illustration. Often, it will be worthwhile to redraft a pattern from one that can only be hand-pieced to one that can be pieced by machine. Or, apply speed-piecing methods to some of these old patterns.

I have included patterns with great possibilities. Some of them are patterns from thirties' newspapers, often redrafted for ease of piecing. A few are patterns from old tops or blocks, origin unknown, and one is my original block. Continue the experimental attitude of the thirties. A collection of old fabrics can be used to make a thirties'-type quilt, or new fabric can be used for a different appeal. Don't forget to sign your quilt and date it. Someone might be fooled otherwise.

THREE ACROSS

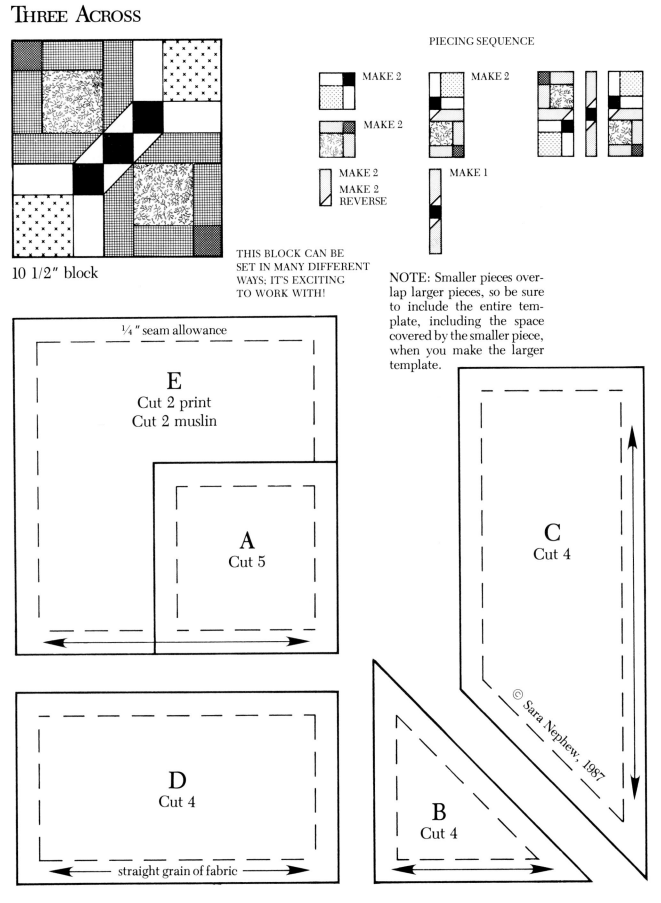

10 1/2″ block

PIECING SEQUENCE

MAKE 2

MAKE 2

MAKE 2

MAKE 2

MAKE 2

MAKE 2
REVERSE

MAKE 1

THIS BLOCK CAN BE
SET IN MANY DIFFERENT
WAYS; IT'S EXCITING
TO WORK WITH!

NOTE: Smaller pieces overlap larger pieces, so be sure
to include the entire template, including the space
covered by the smaller piece,
when you make the larger
template.

¼ ″ seam allowance

E
Cut 2 print
Cut 2 muslin

A
Cut 5

C
Cut 4

© Sara Nephew, 1987

D
Cut 4

straight grain of fabric

B
Cut 4

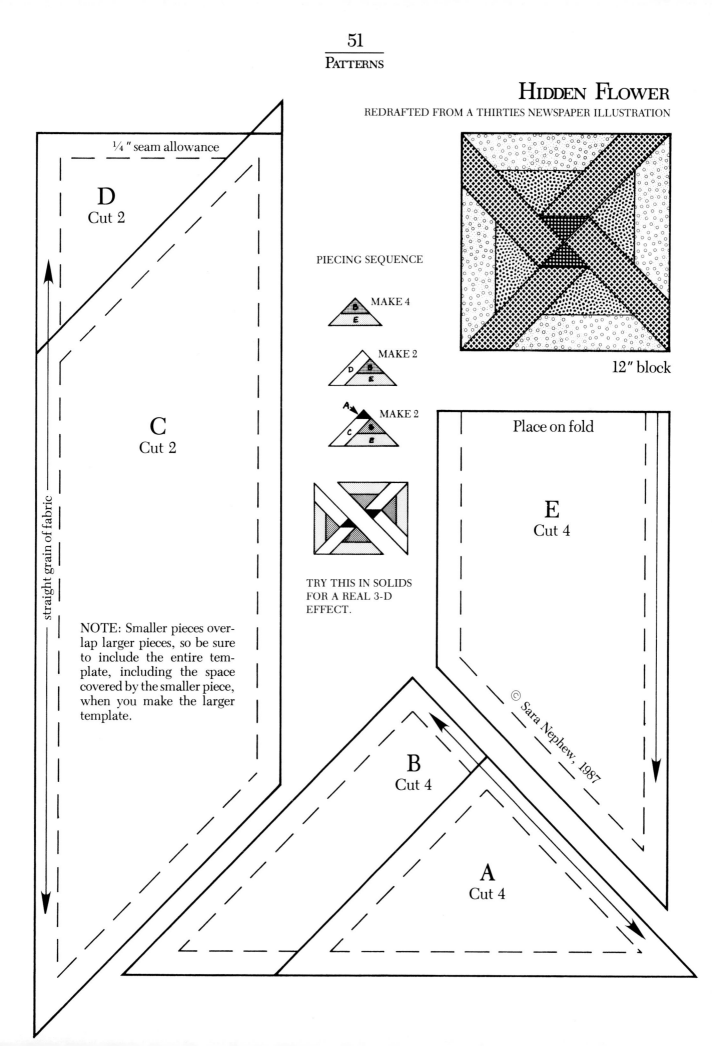

HIDDEN FLOWER
REDRAFTED FROM A THIRTIES NEWSPAPER ILLUSTRATION

¼ " seam allowance

D
Cut 2

C
Cut 2

straight grain of fabric

PIECING SEQUENCE

MAKE 4

MAKE 2

MAKE 2

TRY THIS IN SOLIDS
FOR A REAL 3-D
EFFECT.

12" block

Place on fold

E
Cut 4

© Sara Nephew, 1987

NOTE: Smaller pieces over-lap larger pieces, so be sure to include the entire tem-plate, including the space covered by the smaller piece, when you make the larger template.

B
Cut 4

A
Cut 4

Shooting Star
REDRAFTED FROM A THIRTIES NEWSPAPER ILLUSTRATION

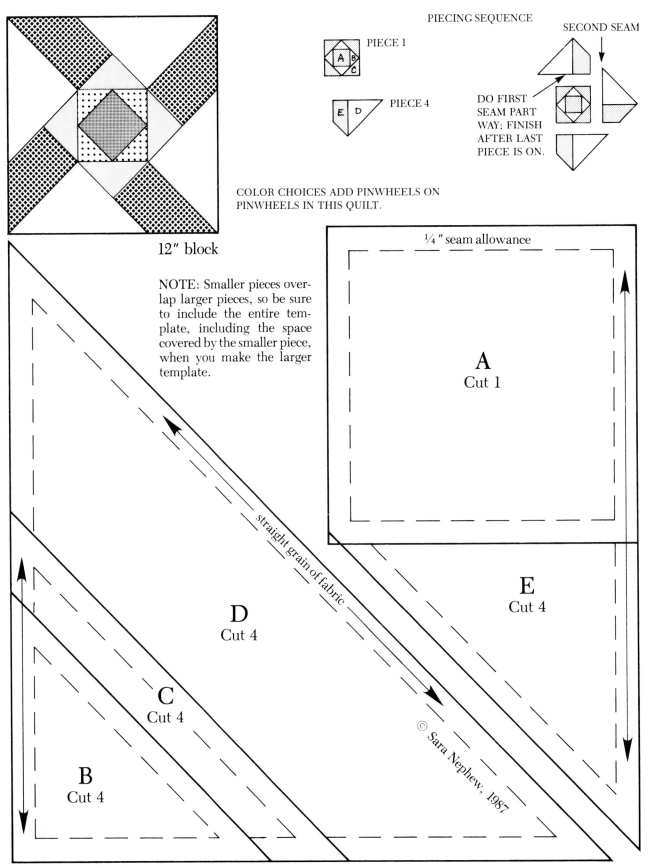

12″ block

PIECING SEQUENCE

PIECE 1

PIECE 4

SECOND SEAM

DO FIRST
SEAM PART
WAY; FINISH
AFTER LAST
PIECE IS ON.

COLOR CHOICES ADD PINWHEELS ON
PINWHEELS IN THIS QUILT.

NOTE: Smaller pieces overlap larger pieces, so be sure
to include the entire template, including the space
covered by the smaller piece,
when you make the larger
template.

¼″ seam allowance

A
Cut 1

E
Cut 4

straight grain of fabric

D
Cut 4

C
Cut 4

B
Cut 4

© Sara Nephew, 1987

PINWHEEL

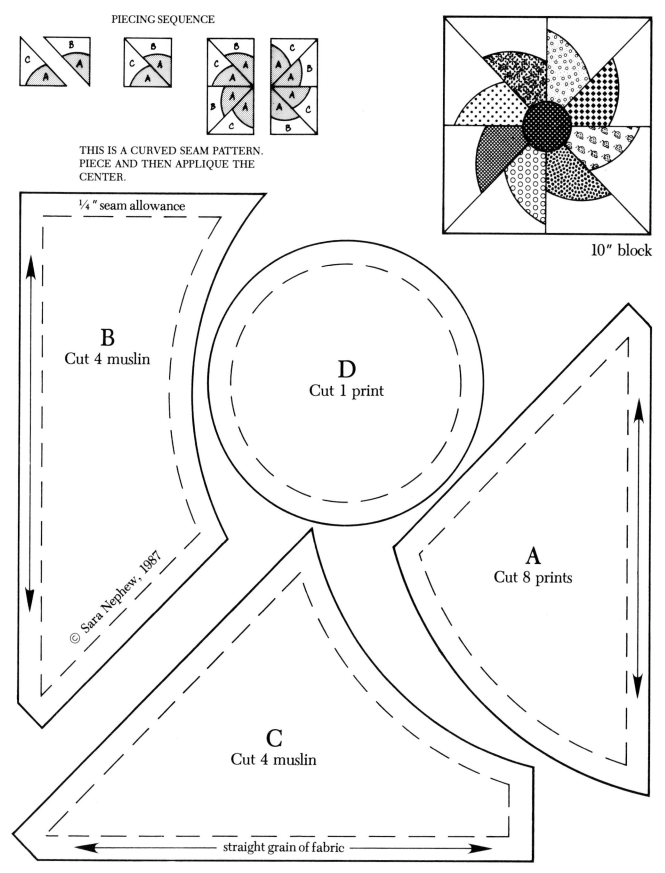

PIECING SEQUENCE

THIS IS A CURVED SEAM PATTERN.
PIECE AND THEN APPLIQUE THE
CENTER.

10" block

¼" seam allowance

B
Cut 4 muslin

© Sara Nephew, 1987

D
Cut 1 print

A
Cut 8 prints

C
Cut 4 muslin

straight grain of fabric

PANSY

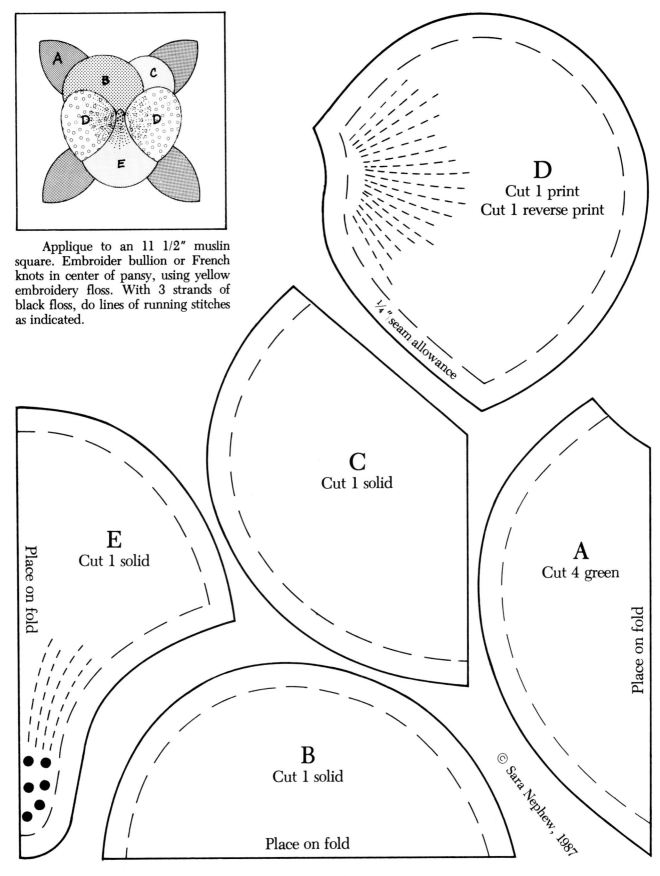

Applique to an 11 1/2″ muslin square. Embroider bullion or French knots in center of pansy, using yellow embroidery floss. With 3 strands of black floss, do lines of running stitches as indicated.

D
Cut 1 print
Cut 1 reverse print

1/4 ″ seam allowance

C
Cut 1 solid

A
Cut 4 green

Place on fold

E
Cut 1 solid

Place on fold

B
Cut 1 solid

Place on fold

© Sara Nephew, 1987

BIAS BUTTERFLY

Place butterfly diagonally on a 12 1/2" muslin square. Baste wings and body in place, turning under seams where indicated. Applique 1/2" bias tape along top of upper wings. (Start with a piece 6 1/2" long and shorten as necessary.) Along bottom and sides of second pair of wings, applique double fold bias tape after trimming off one fold with scissors. (This will leave a narrow bias strip with two seams turned under. Start with a 7" strip and shorten as necessary.) Embroider with pearl cotton, using a double feather stitch on body and both antennae and a cross stitch on bottom edge of upper wings.

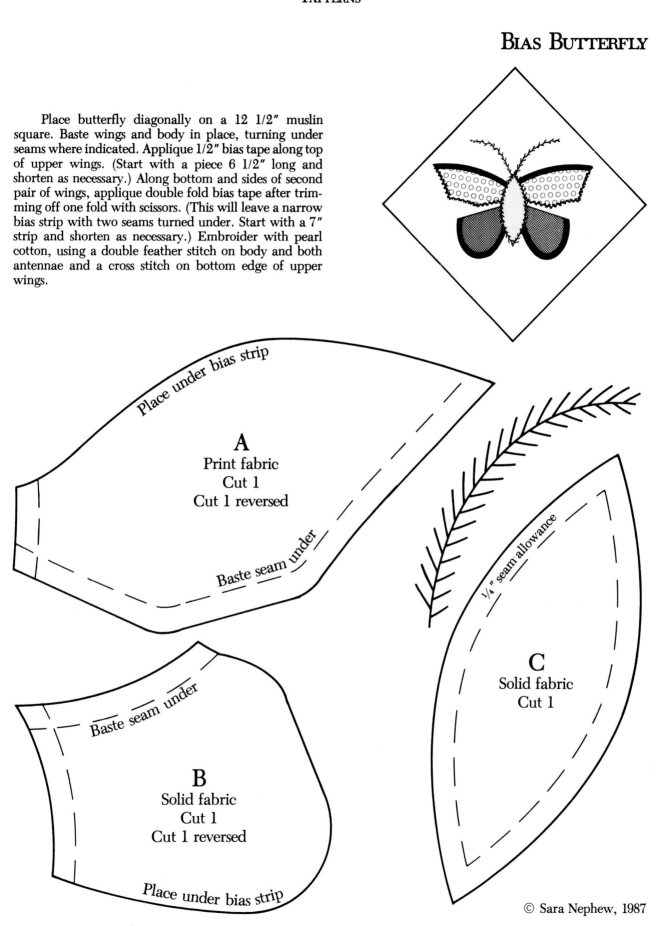

Place under bias strip

A
Print fabric
Cut 1
Cut 1 reversed

Baste seam under

1/4" seam allowance

C
Solid fabric
Cut 1

Baste seam under

B
Solid fabric
Cut 1
Cut 1 reversed

Place under bias strip

© Sara Nephew, 1987

IMPERIAL FAN

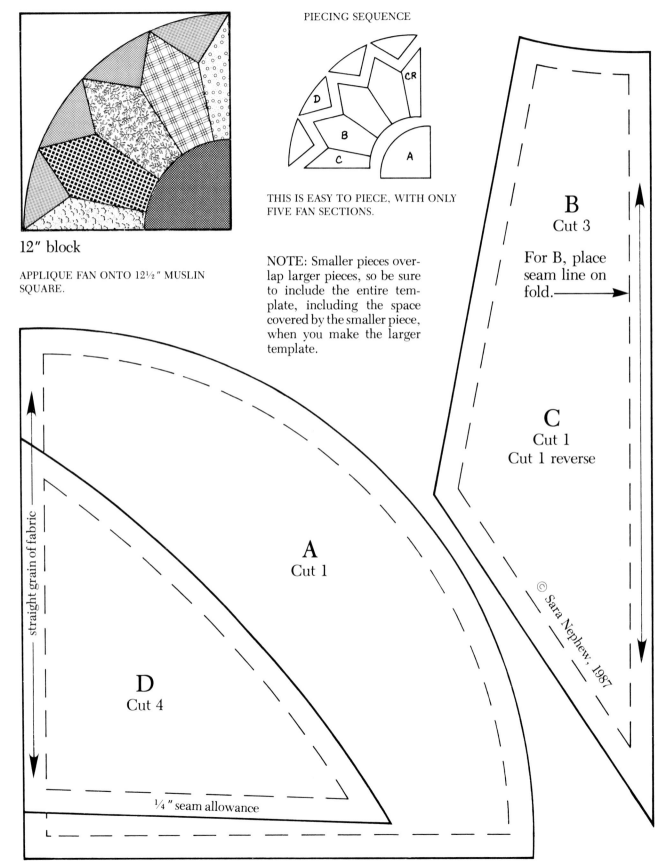

12″ block

APPLIQUE FAN ONTO 12½″ MUSLIN SQUARE.

PIECING SEQUENCE

THIS IS EASY TO PIECE, WITH ONLY FIVE FAN SECTIONS.

NOTE: Smaller pieces overlap larger pieces, so be sure to include the entire template, including the space covered by the smaller piece, when you make the larger template.

B
Cut 3

For B, place seam line on fold. →

C
Cut 1
Cut 1 reverse

© Sara Nephew, 1987

straight grain of fabric

A
Cut 1

D
Cut 4

¼″ seam allowance

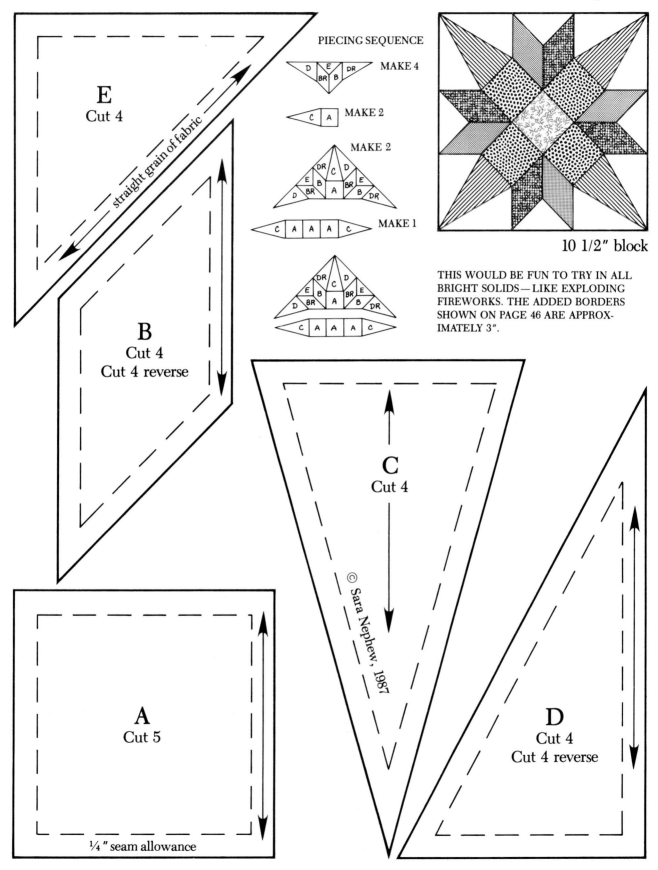

PRAIRIE QUEEN

E
Cut 4

straight grain of fabric

PIECING SEQUENCE

D E DR   MAKE 4
BR B

C A   MAKE 2

DR C D   MAKE 2
E B DR E
D BR A B DR

C A A A C   MAKE 1

DR C D
E B DR E
D BR A B DR
C A A A C

10 1/2" block

THIS WOULD BE FUN TO TRY IN ALL
BRIGHT SOLIDS—LIKE EXPLODING
FIREWORKS. THE ADDED BORDERS
SHOWN ON PAGE 46 ARE APPROX-
IMATELY 3".

B
Cut 4
Cut 4 reverse

C
Cut 4

© Sara Nephew, 1987

D
Cut 4
Cut 4 reverse

A
Cut 5

¼ " seam allowance

RISING SUN
REDRAFTED FROM A THIRTIES NEWSPAPER ILLUSTRATION

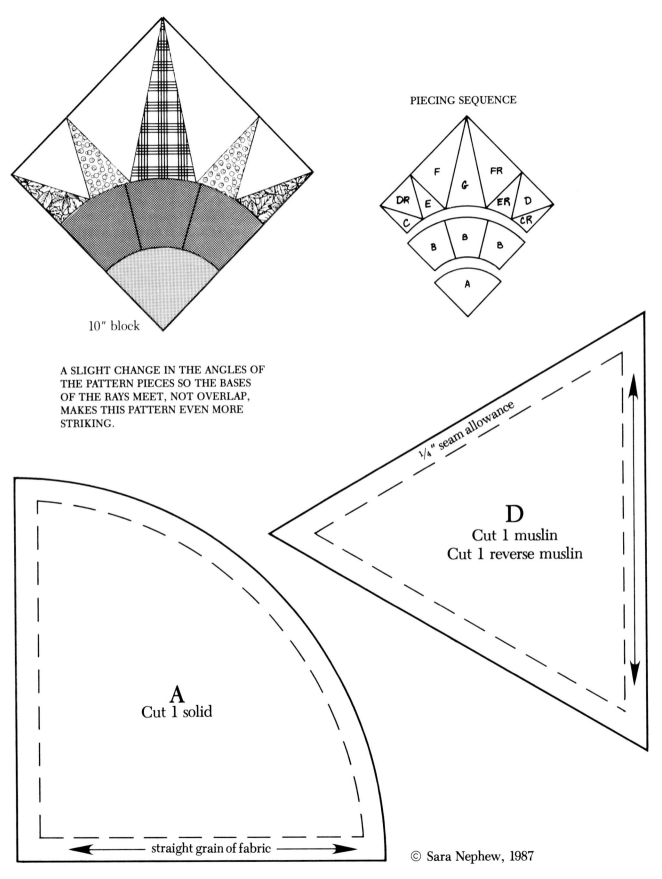

10″ block

PIECING SEQUENCE

A SLIGHT CHANGE IN THE ANGLES OF
THE PATTERN PIECES SO THE BASES
OF THE RAYS MEET, NOT OVERLAP,
MAKES THIS PATTERN EVEN MORE
STRIKING.

¼″ seam allowance

D
Cut 1 muslin
Cut 1 reverse muslin

A
Cut 1 solid

← straight grain of fabric →

© Sara Nephew, 1987

RISING SUN

NOTE: Smaller pieces overlap larger pieces, so be sure to include the entire template, including the space covered by the smaller piece, when you make the larger template.

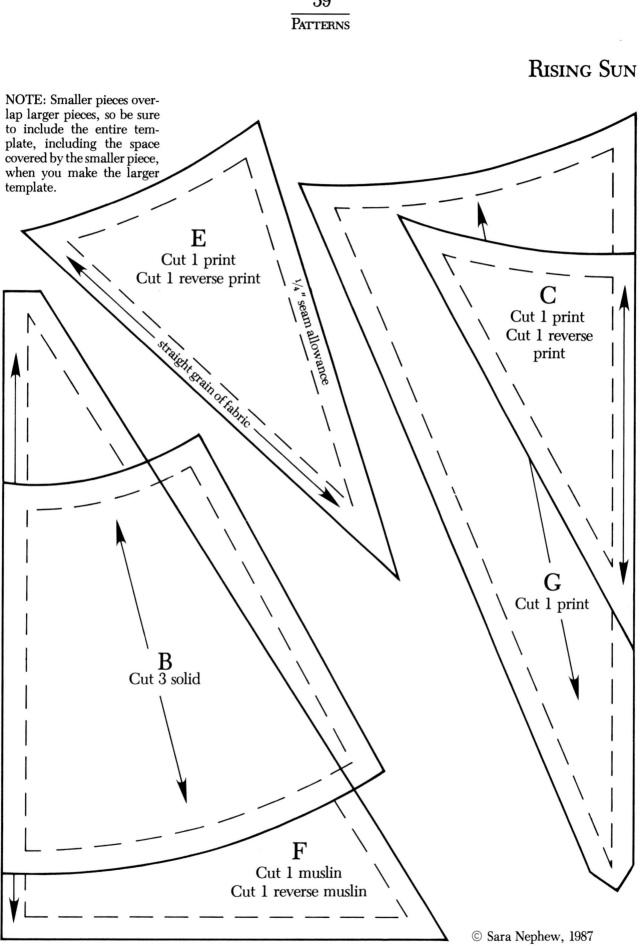

E
Cut 1 print
Cut 1 reverse print

¼" seam allowance

straight grain of fabric

C
Cut 1 print
Cut 1 reverse print

G
Cut 1 print

B
Cut 3 solid

F
Cut 1 muslin
Cut 1 reverse muslin

© Sara Nephew, 1987

ROLLING STONE
REDRAFTED FROM A THIRTIES NEWSPAPER ILLUSTRATION

12″ block

PIECING SEQUENCE

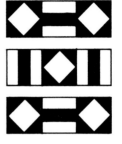

MAKE 4

MAKE 5

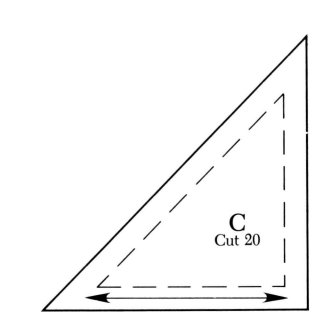

A SIMPLE BLOCK, BUT ONE
WITH POSSIBILITIES.
SPEED-PIECE THE STRIP
UNIT FOR FAST ASSEMBLY.

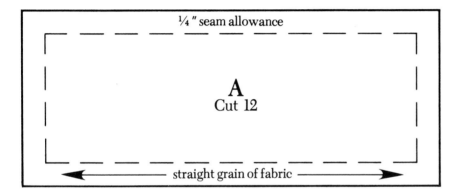

¼″ seam allowance

A
Cut 12

straight grain of fabric

© Sara Nephew, 1987

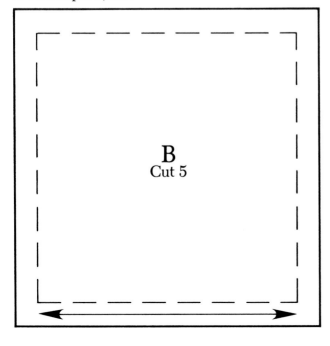

B
Cut 5

C
Cut 20

LOG CHAIN

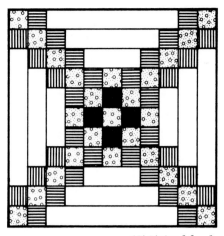

17 7/8" block

SPEED PIECING WOULD MAKE THIS A
VERY FAST QUILT!

PIECING SEQUENCE

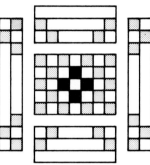

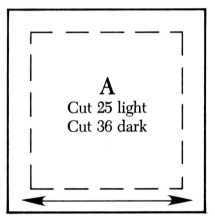

NOTE: Smaller pieces overlap larger pieces, so be sure
to include the entire template, including the space
covered by the smaller piece,
when you make the larger
template.

TRY DIVIDING THIS DIAGONALLY
WITH COLOR AS A LOG CABIN BLOCK
WOULD BE.

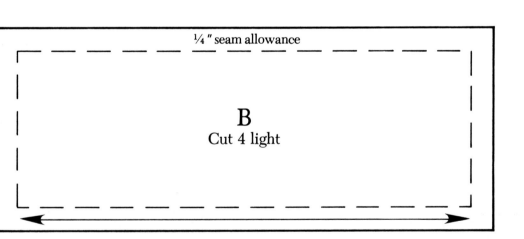

© Sara Nephew, 1987

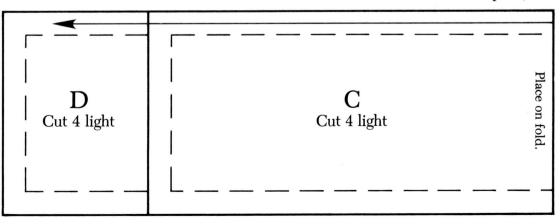

TEA PARTY

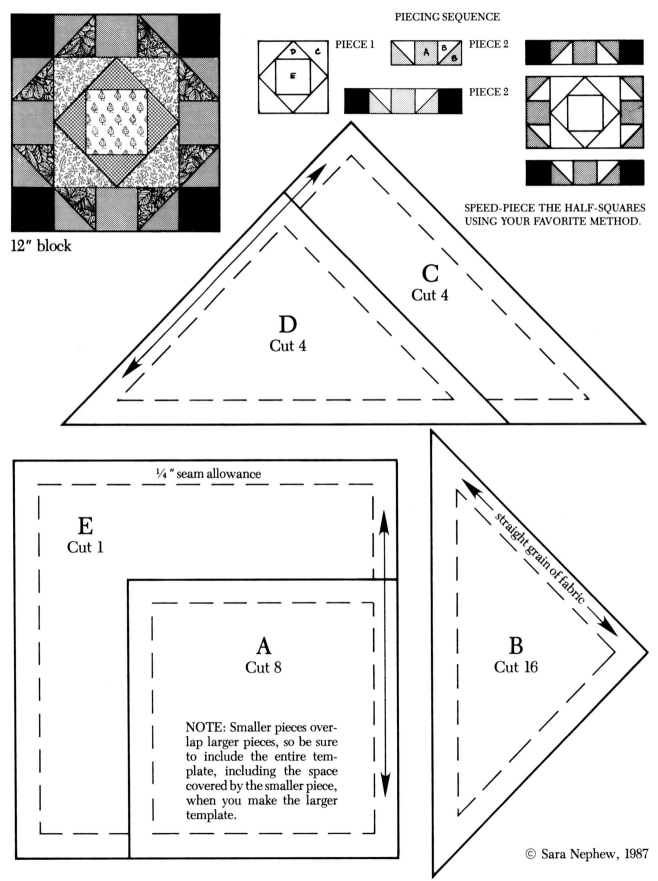

12" block

PIECING SEQUENCE

PIECE 1

PIECE 2

PIECE 2

SPEED-PIECE THE HALF-SQUARES
USING YOUR FAVORITE METHOD.

C
Cut 4

D
Cut 4

¼ " seam allowance

E
Cut 1

A
Cut 8

NOTE: Smaller pieces overlap larger pieces, so be sure
to include the entire template, including the space
covered by the smaller piece,
when you make the larger
template.

B
Cut 16

straight grain of fabric

© Sara Nephew, 1987

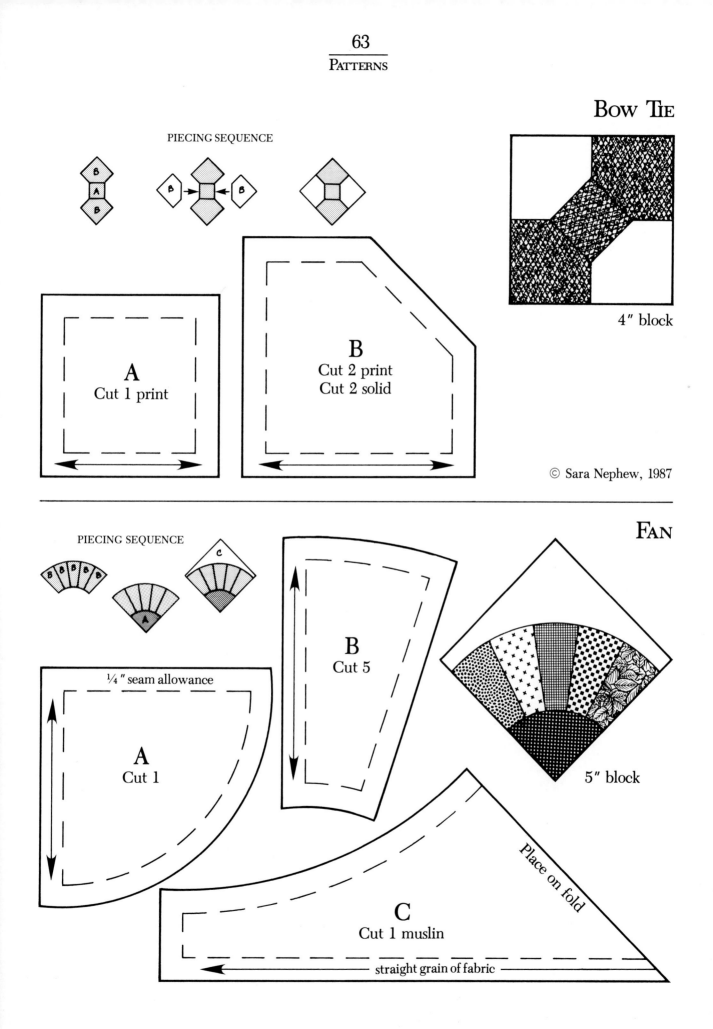

BOW TIE

PIECING SEQUENCE

4″ block

A
Cut 1 print

B
Cut 2 print
Cut 2 solid

© Sara Nephew, 1987

FAN

PIECING SEQUENCE

¼″ seam allowance

A
Cut 1

B
Cut 5

C
Cut 1 muslin

Place on fold

straight grain of fabric

5″ block

BIBLIOGRAPHY

A. B. C. Fabrics. New York: Arthur Bier & Co., Inc., 1929.

Allen, Frederick Lewis. *The Big Change: America Transforms Itself 1900-1950.* New York: Harper & Bros., 1952.

Aronson, Joseph. *The Book of Furniture and Decoration: Period and Modern.* New York: Crown Publishers, 1936.

Barck, Oscar Theodore and Blake, Nelson Maynard. *Since 1900.* New York: Macmillan Co., 1974.

Battersby, Martin. *The Decorative Thirties.* New York: Walker & Co., 1971.

Battersby, Martin. *The Decorative Twenties.* New York: Walker & Co., 1969.

Benberry, Cuesta. "The Twentieth Century's First Quilt Revival: Parts I, II, & III." *Quilter's Newsletter Magazine,* July/Aug., Sept., Oct. 1979.

Brackman, Barbara. "Dating Old Quilts, Parts One, Two, and Three." *Quilter's Newsletter Magazine,* Sept., Oct., Nov. 1984.

Conroy, Mary. *Three Hundred Years of Canada's Quilts.* Toronto: Griffin House, 1976.

Drexler, Arthur and Daniel, Greta. *Introduction to Twentieth Century Design.* New York: Doubleday & Co., 1959.

Gross, Joyce. "Cuesta Benberry: Part II Significant Milestones for Quilters." *Quilter's Journal,* no. 24 (1984), pp. 24-26.

Hagerman, Betty J. *A Meeting of the Sunbonnet Children.* Baldwin City, Kans.: Betty J. Hagerman, 1979.

Kinfolk—A Compilation of Letters, Genealogy, Newspaper Clippings, etc., Relating to the Stuart Family.

Lasansky, Jeanette. *Pieced By Mother: Over One Hundred Years of Quiltmaking Traditions.* Lewisburg, Pa.: Oral Traditions Project, 1987.

"Lois Hartwig's Feedsack Quilts." *Quilter's Newsletter Magazine,* April 1986.

McKim, Ruby. *One Hundred and One Patchwork Patterns.* New York: Dover Publications, Inc., 1962.

McMorris, Penny and Kile, Michael. *The Art Quilt.* San Francisco: Quilt Digest Press, 1986.

Ward's Mid-Winter Super Sale Catalog. Portland: Montgomery Ward & Co., Feb. 28, 1933.

FOOTNOTES

1. Frederick Lewis Allen, *The Big Change,* p. 99.
2. Ibid., p. 106.
3. Oscar Theodore Barck & Nelson Maynard Blake, *Since 1900,* p. 229.
4. Betty J. Hagerman, *A Meeting of the Sunbonnet Children,* p. 7.
5. Jeanette Lasansky, *Pieced By Mother,* p. 106.
6. Ibid., p. 107.

THAT PATCHWORK PLACE PUBLICATIONS

Back to Square One by Nancy J. Martin	15.95
Bearwear by Nancy J. Martin	7.95
Branching Out—Tree Quilts by Carolann Palmer	11.95
Cathedral Window—A New View by Mary Ryder Kline	6.00
Christmas Classics by Sue Saltkill	6.95
Christmas Memories—A Folk Art Celebration by Nancy J. Martin	14.95
Christmas Quilts by Marsha McCloskey	11.95
Copy Art For Quilters by Nancy J. Martin	6.95
Dozen Variables by Marsha McCloskey and Nancy J. Martin	15.95
Feathered Star Quilts by Marsha McCloskey	17.95
Happy Endings: Finishing the Edges of Your Quilt by Mimi Dietrich	6.95
Holiday Happenings by Christal Carter	14.95
Housing Projects by Nancy J. Martin	9.95
Make a Medallion by Kathy Cook	12.95
More Template-Free Quiltmaking by Trudie Hughes	12.95
Pieces of the Past by Nancy J. Martin	18.95
Projects for Blocks and Borders by Marsha McCloskey	14.95
Quilter's Christmas by Nancyann Twelker	11.95
Quilts from a Different Angle by Sara Nephew	8.95
Sew Special by Susan A. Grosskopf	6.00
Small Quilts by Marsha McCloskey	6.00
Stencil Patch by Nancy J. Martin	6.00
Template-Free Quiltmaking by Trudie Hughes	12.95
Wall Quilts by Marsha McCloskey	8.00